TIMBER PRESS
POCKET GUIDE TO
Japanese Maples

TIMBER PRESS
POCKET GUIDE TO

Japanese Maples

J. D. VERTREES
with Peter Gregory

TIMBER PRESS
PORTLAND • LONDON

Frontispiece: *Acer palmatum* 'Saoshika'. Photo by Daniel Otis.

All photos copyright of the individual photographers. Photos by J. D. Vertrees used by permission of the Estate of J. D. Vertrees, courtesy of Oregon State University Archives, Corvallis.

Published in 2007 by Timber Press, Inc.

The Haseltine Building
133 S.W. Second Avenue, Suite 450
Portland, Oregon 97204-3527, U.S.A.
www.timberpress.com

2 The Quadrant
135 Salusbury Road
London NW6 6RJ
United Kingdom
www.timberpress.co.uk

Third printing 2008

Printed through Colorcraft Ltd., Hong Kong

Library of Congress Cataloging-in-Publication Data

Vertrees, J. D.
  Timber Press pocket guide to Japanese maples / J. D. Vertrees with
Peter Gregory.
        p. cm.
  Includes bibliographical references and index.
  ISBN-13: 978-0-88192-799-3
  1. Japanese maple. I. Gregory, Peter, 1929- II. Title.
  SB413.J34V48 2007
  635.9'77378—dc22
                      2006017442

A catalog record for this book is also available from the British Library.

Dedication

To Roseann—
Without her unselfish encouragement, wisdom, and devotion, none of this would have been possible.

—JDV

Acknowledgments

My thanks go once again, to everyone mentioned in the third edition of *Japanese Maples*, on which this volume is based, and to the many maple collectors and growers worldwide who sent me cultivar lists and catalogs—far too numerous to mention individually. My special thanks to Talon Buchholz, Nancy Fiers, and Karan Junker for their valuable advice and for so freely sharing their considerable knowledge, experience, and photographs with me.

Also to my talented photographic friends Cor van Gelderen, Harold Greer, Andrea Jones, the late Harry Olsen, Daniel Otis, and Francis Schroeder for generously offering so many of their beautiful photographs. The kindness of maple enthusiasts Robert Jamgochian of Mendocino Maples Nursery (Mendocino, California), Douglas Justice of the University of British Columbia Botanical Garden (Vancouver, Canada), and Ray Prag of Forestfarm (Williams, Oregon) in providing photographs is also very much appreciated.

—PG

About This Book

The plant entries in this pocket guide are divided into two sections: the first including only cultivars of *Acer palmatum*, the true Japanese maple, and the second for other species and cultivars which are cultivated in Japan. Within each of these sections, plants are arranged in alphabetical order by scientific name.

The descriptions indicate the likely mature size of a plant grown under normal garden conditions and care. The eventual height and spread of a specific maple, however, will vary according to the conditions in which it is grown—temperature, moisture, fertility, exposure, soil pH, competition, care, pruning, in a container or in the garden, and so forth.

In normal garden conditions, most Japanese maples can grow in USDA hardiness zones 5 through 9, so again, to avoid endless repetition, this information was omitted from the individual plant descriptions. In a few cases, however, plants are noted as being "tender." Such maples are best grown in USDA zones 6 through 9.

CONTENTS

Opposite: When viewed with sunlight filtering through them,
maple leaves display brilliant coloring. Photo by Peter Gregory.

PREFACE

When Oregon nurseryman J. D. Vertrees (1915–1993) originally wrote *Japanese Maples* in the 1970s, he wanted to provide a comprehensive source of information on the culture, identification, and nomenclature of this large group of cultivars. He also intended to reduce confusion and bring stability to the naming of these plants. That his volume has become an invaluable reference book, the bible for maple growers and enthusiasts worldwide, is a measure of its success in achieving these objectives.

Since that time considerably more cultivars have become available. In 2001, I had the privilege of updating Mr. Vertrees' text, adding information about the many worthwhile introductions and bringing the botanical and nomenclatural information into line with current knowledge. The resulting third edition of *Japanese Maples* continues to be the foremost reference book on the subject.

Now it is again my privilege to collaborate in the preparation of a portable companion to that work, a pocket guide to a wonderfully versatile group of woody plants, which are more varied in their uses, shapes, sizes, and colors throughout the year than almost any other group of garden plants. This guide provides practical information on the selection, siting, planting, and aftercare of species and cultivars alike and contains lists of suggested plants for particular situations and purposes. The main portion of the book consists of brief descriptions and illustrations of more than 300 widely available cultivars. These are followed by maps of the hardiness zones for North America and Europe, a list of retail suppliers who carry a good range of these plants, plus recommended books for further information.

Peter Gregory

Opposite: *Acer palmatum* 'Villa Taranto'. Photo by Harold Greer.

INTRODUCTION

The term "Japanese maple" has two meanings. In horticulture, it generally refers to only *Acer palmatum* and its cultivars. Other maples that grow in Japan are referred to as "maples from Japan." In botany, however, the term "Japanese maple" embraces all 23 *Acer* species that grow wild on the Japanese islands.

In the present volume, the term is used in its botanical sense to indicate maples that are native to Japan, but plant descriptions have been divided into two sections. The first includes only *Acer palmatum* and its cultivars. A second, smaller listing of maple descriptions includes other maples grown in Japan.

Although many maple species have very colorful flowers, they are not thought of as flowering plants. Rather, they are known for their great variation in leaf color and shape, especially in the spring. Nothing more closely resembles a flowering shrub than the various cultivars of *Acer palmatum* with their vibrant spring leaves. Among these are 'Higasa yama' with popcorn-like emerging leaves in bright yellows and pink-reds, 'Corallinum' with eye-catching pink-red spring leaves, 'Katsura' with vivid orange-yellow spring color, and 'Beni shichihenge' with variegated pink-green leaves—all lasting for several weeks into early summer.

During summer, the leaf color varies from soft yellow-green to deep green and from orange-red to deep purple-red. These hues are augmented by numerous variegations in white, cream, and yellow, adding color to any landscape. Group plantings of maples in the proper setting, especially of those with lacy leaves, offer unusual brilliance and delicacy. Combinations of lacelike tracery of form, plus crimson, maroon, green-red, or variegated white-green-pink tones blend in the most pleasing way with the delicate cascading form of the plant.

Following the spring show is the spectacular explosion of fall color for which maples are famous. It ranges from the dramatic, almost fluorescent, crimson flame display of *Acer palmatum* 'Ōsakazuki', the mixtures of green, yellow, orange, scarlet, and crimson of most *A. japonicum* cultivars, the golds of *A. palmatum* 'Shishigashira', and the bright yellows flushed with oranges and pinks of *A. shirasawanum* 'Aureum'. Fall color is an inherent characteristic of most maples, brought on by lowering temperatures, shorter days, and stronger drying winds, which hasten the hardening off and leaf-fall process in preparation for winter. These colors can be enhanced by reducing a plant's water supply and by withholding fertilizer, especially if it contains nitrates.

In addition to the spectrum of changing colors every year, maples present such a wide range of

The colorful emerging leaves of *Acer palmatum* 'Higasa yama'. Photo by Peter Gregory.

Opposite: *Acer sieboldianum*. Photo by Peter Gregory.

sizes that there can be "a plant for every occasion." Some cultivars form tall, upright trees up to 33 ft. (10 m). These will fit in the garden landscape as accent plants, shade for smaller understory plants, outline plantings along driveways and walks, interplantings with other similarly sized plants in naturalized landscapes, or as outstanding specimen plants holding forth with their own importance.

Medium-sized selections offer all the uses listed for their taller counterparts, and they can also be interplanted with rhododendrons and other flowering shrubs to provide variety and color. The magnificent cascading group of maples, including the lace-leaved cultivars, works well in mixed plantings. Numerous forms of smaller plants add great interest also. They naturally shape themselves into space-saving plants and, with additional shaping and pruning, can be established in limited areas.

The great variety of dwarf maple cultivars opens up numerous possibilities. The first is bonsai culture, for which maples are ideally suited, though any form or size of *Acer palmatum* or *A. japonicum* adapts well to bonsai culture. Dwarf maples are also ideal for the front of shrub borders, anywhere in alpine gardens, and among herbaceous perennials, annuals, and bulbs. They excel as accent plants in secluded nooks or bold sites in an informal landscape. These smaller maples illustrate choices for small garden landscape plantings as well as for patio and container growing.

Suffice it to say that the wide variation in leaf size, form, color, and texture as well as plant size, shape, and vigor make it possible to find something to fill virtually any need in the garden or containerized patio.

Variegation

Variegation in maple leaves occurs when one or more contrasting colors are paired with the basic green or red color. The contrasting color can be white, cream, yellow, light green, gray-green, black, pink, or red. The variegation may dominate almost to obscure the green, as in the almost white-leaved *Acer crataegifolium* 'Veitchii',

or it may occur only in splashes on occasional leaves, as in the red-leaved *A. palmatum* 'Yūbae'. The variegation may be in the form of dots, speckles, stripes, splashes, or reticulations (netting) with the veins a contrasting color as in *A. palmatum* 'Shigitatsu sawa'.

Variegated cultivars can revert to all green or all red. This color change can happen on vigorous shoots and especially if plants are overfertilized or grown in very fertile conditions. Hence, variegated plants should not be overfed. Most variegates also need some shade or protection from afternoon sun.

Culture in the Garden

Japanese maples are hardy and remarkably adaptable to soil and climatic conditions. *Acer palmatum* and *A. japonicum* have adapted to a wide range of environments in their native Japan. In North America, they thrive from the rainforest conditions of the Pacific Northwest to the very warm climate of Southern California, from Upstate New York down the Atlantic Seaboard to the Southeast and through the Midwest. In Europe, they grow in the warm Mediterranean conditions of Italy, the almost-pure peat soils of Boskoop, Netherlands, and the varied soils in Britain. They also thrive in many parts of Australasia. Thus we begin to understand the versatility of these ornamentals.

Maples are widely used as specimen plants and companion plants. Most upright cultivars of *Acer palmatum* and *A. japonicum* attain a height of 26–30 ft. (8–9 m) in 50 years, depending upon site and conditions. Many, especially the dissectums, mature as large shrubs at 16 ft. (5 m) or less, while mature cultivars in the Dwarf Group rarely exceed 6$\frac{1}{2}$ ft. (2 m).

The green varieties take full sun very well. In extremely hot situations, they may sunburn slightly. Afternoon shade aids in preventing this, as does an adequate water supply. Variegated leaf forms need semishade or at least protection from the blistering afternoon sun. The red dissectums appreciate some shade but cannot develop their typical deep red colors without benefit of full sunlight for at least part of the day. In general, the color of most red cultivars is greatly enhanced in full sun, and some forms (such as *Acer palmatum* 'Fior d'Arancio') readily revert to green in too much shade.

Use in the Garden Landscape

Using maples in the garden is a challenge because there are so many different types, colors, shapes, and growth rates from which to choose. This very fact makes it easier for homeowners to create whatever mood or effect is desired.

Dissectums

A familiar form of the Japanese maple is the dissectum, or laceleaf. It occurs with red or green foliage and is commonly offered in most retail nurseries. Dissectums are outstanding as individual specimen plants, container trees for the patio, accent plants in lawns, companion plants in a mixed border, or in a special spot in the rock garden. They are particularly showy accent plants when sited beside a pool, overhanging running water, or in prominent spots along a winding path. Properly cared for old specimen plants possess a magnificent stateliness. After leaf fall, the characteristic shapely and twisting branch scaffolding carries the featured beauty on through the winter, especially if the dead leaves and debris are cleaned out of the interior.

Young plants can grow rapidly at first, during which time they can be trained in shape and structure to make good accent plants. They have a natural tendency not to become too large; however, the "cute little plant" purchased as a starter should be allowed plenty of room to spread, so that it can grow into the typical cascading mushroom shape which is so desirable.

Upright Growers

The upright forms present a great number of choices and landscaping possibilities. Some offer bright spring color while others have stunning fall

Acer palmatum 'Kihachijō' and *A. palmatum* 'Nuresagi' are excellent companions for fall color. Photo by J. D. Vertrees.

color. Their shapes vary from tall to spreading to cascading, but all can easily be pruned to the desired shape. Some cultivars develop unusual limb structures for winter enjoyment; others (*Acer palmatum* 'Sango kaku') have brightly colored winter shoots and branches or a unique corky bark (*A. palmatum* 'Arakawa').

An individual large accent plant that is situated in a prominent place attracts attention from every part of the garden, whether it has red (*Acer palmatum* 'Bloodgood'), green (*A. palmatum* 'Autumn Glory'), or variegated leaves (*A. palmatum* 'Butterfly'). For group plantings, a blending of several color types forms an ever-changing canopy throughout the seasons.

Large upright forms are useful as overstory plants for alpine, rock garden, or flower borders; as solid plantings employing several types to make a "woodsy" grove; as a border for the background edge of a garden landscape by adding various colors and textures; or as a cor-

ner or end specimen to emphasize a change in landscape design or use.

These maples readily adapt to a range of cultural situations. They adjust to the needs of various companion plants, from acid-loving rhododendrons, azaleas, kalmias, and dwarf conifers to a great variety of perennials and bulbs. Maples also blend well with shrubs and perennials which prefer slight-to-medium alkaline soils, but they will not tolerate highly alkaline soils. Raised beds or container growing is the answer in such cases. These maples do not have a strongly invasive root system and root competition is not vicious. So Japanese maples are compatible with most plants and do not damage borders or paths.

Mass Plantings

For larger gardens, mass plantings offer tremendous possibilities, such as two or more outstanding cultivars or species for each season, which can provide interest throughout the year. For

Acer palmatum f. *dissectum* in a mixed border. Photo by J. D. Vertrees.

early color, combine cultivars from the spring-flowering and variegated groups. For summer color, blend red- and green-leaved forms. For stunning fall color, plant crimson-leaved *Acer palmatum* 'Ōsakazuki' with orange-leaved *A. palmatum* 'Hōgyoku'. To prolong interest through the winter, grow cultivars with warty bark and colored shoots.

Bright red cultivars can be sited so that the sunlight filters through the foliage with spectacular effect. Weeping dissectums can be blended with various dwarf forms to visually tie the planting to the ground. A hedge of red or green dissectums can make a distinctive garden boundary. A mixture of red and green forms, covering a range of autumn colors, could make an unusual and impressive impact.

Mass planting of just one plant type is usually unwise, however, as this can be monotonous, especially in the winter. Interplanting maples with dwarf conifers and low-growing rhododendrons, camellias, kalmias, and other evergreen shrubs helps break up such monotony.

Containers

Japanese maples can be successfully grown in containers. Container planting is well-suited to small gardens and landscapes as well as patio gardening. With proper but not overdemanding care, maples can be grown in containers for several years without repotting or root pruning. Dwarf types in ornamental urns are ideal for small patios. Where larger containers can be utilized, the range of choices increases greatly. Not only can the dwarf forms be grown singly or in small groupings, but also the larger-growing dissectums and the upright cultivars do extremely well. The choice of form, color, leaf texture, and winter branching is unlimited.

Full-sized maples grow well in tubs or large permanent containers. Their fibrous roots enable them to utilize the limited area without root binding and choking themselves too easily. Occasional directive shaping or pruning is not a demanding chore, attention possibly once or twice a season being required.

Two important requirements must be met in all container planting. First, the planting mixture must be open enough to allow good drainage and aeration, and not become waterlogged. Most commercial composts, such as rose or ericaceous composts, are adequate. Second, the containers must be given regular attention and not neglected during the growing season, such as during a vacation. Minimal fertilization is necessary to maintain good color, and regular but moderate watering is required. Overwatering can be detrimental, but so can lack of watering during long dry spells. Unlike the roots of open-ground plants, the roots of container plants cannot search further afield for moisture.

In cold climates, some protection of the roots is necessary. Wrapping in poly-foam sheets, in turn covered by burlap, is effective for large containers. Smaller containers can be set in beds of mulch. The mulching should cover the containers to about 2 in. (5 cm) above the container top. In mild winters, an occasional cold snap may cause some twig dieback if the plants have not hardened-off properly. This natural pruning is of no great consequence.

In areas of extreme winters, the tops of the plants should be protected from strong freezing winds which rapidly desiccate the bark and cambium. Bracken or straw wrapped loosely round the trunk affords effective protection in most cases.

Planting

Maples are easy to plant. They have a relatively shallow fibrous root system, not a deep tap root. Regular watering helps maintain the roots in the upper soil levels. This shallow rooting allows planting in soils which may have a hard stratum or bedrock close to the surface. With adequate root coverage and attention to uniform moisture supply, these plants do an excellent job of beautifying difficult areas. I cannot overstress the uniformity of watering—not large amounts, but rather constant amounts.

The planting hole should be slightly larger than the plant's root mass. To enable the root system to establish itself quickly, mix organic compost with the soil, that is, composted conifer bark mulch, rhododendron planting mix, or rose compost. Never use sawdust or wood chippings as, during their breakdown, they use up the available soil nitrogen.

The planting hole should always be prepared in advance, so that the plant roots are not exposed to drying out longer than is necessary. The hole should be deep enough to allow the plant's root collar to be level with the surface. The plant roots should be spread out in the planting hole bottom and, as the soil is replaced, it should be gently firmed with the foot, so that the finer root hairs are not left in pockets of air. In heavy soils, such as clay, success will be greater if the hole is shallow so that the root system is partly above the ground level. When filling in the hole, the soil should then be mounded up to the root collar to protect the roots from drying out. Planting maples in deep holes in heavy soil is like planting them in large iron kettles with no drainage. The plant will soon drown and die.

Whatever the soil conditions, the tree should never be planted deeper than the root collar. After the first few seasons, the plant will find the level of root activity at which it can exist in particular soil conditions. Maples have been observed growing in some surprisingly dry, shallow, and exposed conditions.

Mulching

Mulching serves several useful purposes—to maintain weed-free conditions, to minimize water loss in dry spells, and to provide winter protection for the roots. A newly planted maple needs several years before its relatively shallow root system is successfully established. The competition from grass roots is especially intense. Hence, the area around a newly planted maple should be kept weed-free for the first two to three years, until the young plant is well-established. Once the area is weed-free, mulching can keep it that way.

When established, the shoots of most Japanese maples can withstand winter freezing and air temperatures down to 0°F (−18°C) and below. When planted normally in the soil, maples can withstand extreme temperatures because the roots are protected sufficiently in the deeper soil. The roots of newly planted trees, however, are less resistant, hence the importance of correct mulching.

The ideal mulch is a 2-in. (5-cm) layer of coarse wood-free bark with an average chip size of about $3/4$ in. (2 cm). It allows moisture downwards but not upwards, it encourages the free exchange of gases, it deters weeds from developing because of the lack of moisture in the upper mulch layers, and it acts as a protective insulating layer during cold winters. Other suitable mulch materials and compromises, such as mulch mats, are available, but bear in mind the absorbency, porosity, weeding, and insulating requirements.

Soils

The ideal soil for Japanese maples is a slightly acid sandy loam with a low to medium amount of organic matter. The acid or neutral soils in which rhododendrons do well seem to be equally suitable for maples. Nonetheless, maples adapt well on less-than-perfect soils of most types.

The site must be reasonably well-drained. Japanese maples do not like wet or swampy conditions, but may be grown along pools and little streams provided the root zones have sufficient drainage and aeration. Growing Japanese maples in containers or raised beds offers alternative choices where impossible soil conditions exist, such as extremely alkaline or acid soils. Soils of an extremely sandy nature will benefit by incorporating organic matter, plus mulching, to help in water retention.

Moisture

Japanese maples do not have any unusual moisture requirement. Grown as companions with most other shrubs and perennials, they are carried along nicely with normal irrigation. The principal water requirement is a uniform supply. If the plant is in a dry situation, it should not be flooded with water at irregular intervals and, if it is grown where moisture is plentiful, it should not be left to dry out during dry spells but should be watered during such times.

The main danger to guard against is very wet periods followed by very dry periods or vice versa. A common cause of leaf scorch is an excessively dry period, even if only a few days, in a normally watered situation. Watering the leaves in full sun during the hot summer months causes another leaf-scorch problem, especially with container-grown specimens. Watering in early morning or early evening prevents this.

Containers must not be allowed to get water-logged, as overwatering can be worse than under-watering. Aeration is as important as irrigation because the roots must be able to breathe. The grower must determine the water requirement of a particular medium and adjust watering accordingly. Proper water management is even more important than type of soil or fertilizer!

Whatever the situation, the water supply, whether little or much, should be constant.

Fertilizing

Japanese maples are not greedy. If the soil is fertile enough for most garden plants, maples will do well. In soils of the northwestern United States, *Acer palmatum* seems to resent the ammonium sources of nitrogen. Calcium nitrate works best, with other non-ammonium sources also working well. A balanced garden fertilizer, such as recommended for roses, applied lightly in early spring, but not more than once a year, provides for these plants.

On very poor soils and in problem areas, a balanced fertilizer for shrubs and trees may be used. A once-a-year early spring application, before the leaves emerge, is generally best. Newer slow-release fertilizer mixes now on the market work well. Old barnyard manure is rich in many nutrients but may need addition of nitrates, introduces

Acer palmatum 'Garyū' growing on a rock. Photo by J. D. Vertrees.

weed seeds, and loses moisture in hot, dry spells. Many variegated cultivars tend to lose their variegation when given excess fertilizer.

Pruning

Where large plants and great expanses allow, it is magnificent to permit these trees to grow unhindered; however, unless one wants to have a large Japanese maple, top shaping and pruning should be started early and considered each year. The smaller the pruning wound, the quicker it will heal. Major pruning should be done during the dormant season, from late autumn to midwinter, before the sap starts rising. Corrective pruning and training can be done at any time of the year, except when the sap is rising and all the plant's energy is devoted to the development of the young leaves.

Cuts should be made just beyond a pair of buds on the twig. Usually, this will then produce two side shoots. When removing a larger limb, the cut should be made *just above* the branch collar—the ridge or line where the branch joins an older branch or stem. Never cut below this natural barrier against the ingress of disease from a pruning wound. Cutting beyond this point not only gets behind the plant's last line of defense, it also creates an even bigger wound surface for disease to attack. Avoid leaving an unnecessarily long "stub," as it provides a food source for disease to build up the strength to penetrate the tree's natural defense system.

The need for *sharp* pruning tools cannot be overemphasized. A clean pruning wound heals much more quickly than a jagged, torn wound created by blunt tools, and the wound calluses over more effectively. To prevent spreading disease from tree to tree, it is good practice to clean and sterilize pruning tools regularly. The use of tree-wound paint on cut surfaces is not recom-

Pruning can shape a Japanese maple for dramatic effects. Photo by Peter Gregory.

mended. Allowing the wound to dry out discourages the germination of disease spores. Painting the pruning wound prevents drying out, and the spores, which are inevitably already on the wood surface, can live like lords, well-protected from the elements and with ample moisture and food on which to thrive.

The fine, twiggy growth in some larger maples should be removed, especially from cultivars in the Dissectum Group, allowing a display of the plant's graceful and intricate structure. The cascading, undulating, and twisting branches in this group can be as beautiful and interesting as the foliage during the winter months. In the case of *Acer palmatum* 'Sango kaku' (coral-red shoots) and *A. palmatum* 'Aoyagi' (bright green shoots), the bark or shoot color is the outstanding feature and should be exposed.

In gardens with limited space, judicious pruning and shaping helps maples to fulfill their purpose and make good specimen plants. It would be nice to own unlimited areas, but most of us are not that fortunate. Pruning and shaping is the answer.

Insect Pests

Japanese maples are rarely subject to serious insect infestations beyond the range of insects normally found in any garden. These include various aphids, mites, and worms (caterpillars). Thrips, leaf hoppers, scale insects, leaf miner flies, and leaf-cutter bees are occasional pests. All can spoil the appearance of the leaves—significantly so in the case of an aphid explosion—but the general health and vigor of the trees are not affected. Root weevils, such as the strawberry root weevil or vine weevil, kill the roots of young trees with the subsequent death of the plants. They are mainly a nursery problem but can also affect container-grown plants.

Aphids. These small sap-sucking insects feed along the veins on the undersides of leaves and on soft, newly emerged young shoot tips. Occasionally they occur in great numbers in mid to late spring following a relatively mild winter. The excretion of the feeding aphids is the "honeydew"

causing unsightly but harmless black sooty molds. Although such molds are usually barely noticeable, they may spoil the appearance of choice maples. Their harmful effect on the trees' future health and growth is minimal. An aphid spray for the garden, such as that used for roses, is usually an adequate control. It must be applied from below to the leaf undersides. The treatment is especially effective if the infestation is anticipated and the spraying is carried out as soon as the first aphids are spotted and repeated two to three times at four- to seven-day intervals.

Mites. More unusual are the occasional infestations of spider mites. A hand lens is needed to see these minute "spiders" which, like aphids, also suck the sap from leaves. They cause speckled yellowish areas along the leaf veins and, if a plant is badly infested, it can become defoliated as the leaves dry up, shrivel, brown, and drop off. Generally, spider mites can only successfully attack already sick trees, those under stress through growing in unsuitable conditions, and in times of moisture stress.

Sometimes, spraying the leaves with water each day and increasing irrigation to the plant offer some relief. Mite-control chemicals are available; however, the only effective control is to plant and maintain maples in suitable growing conditions, and provide an adequate watering routine.

Worms (caterpillars). Leaves are again the target of "worms," wasps, bees, and beetles (such as the Japanese beetle), which chew holes in the leaves and around the edges. However, the larvae of certain moths and butterflies—the "worms" or caterpillars—do most of this kind of damage. Usually these pests do only scattered damage on Japanese maples and are not a sufficient problem to cause concern.

Some of the leaf-chewing larvae belong to the leaf-roller moth. The larva spins a web which rolls the leaf together, so that it can feed in the protective enclosure. These pests are difficult to control with sprays unless a wetting agent (surfactant), such as soft soap, is added. For small areas, handpicking is effective. Gardeners experiencing

Japanese maples blend in well with most trees, in a variety of growing conditions. Photo by Peter Gregory.

serious or repeated problems with these leaf-eating larvae may need to use chemical sprays which cover the insect or leave a deposit on the foliage which the insect takes in as it feeds. In most instances, the damage is minor and scattered, and controls are unnecessary.

Diseases and Other Problems

One of the most talked about and least understood problems of Japanese maples is twig dieback, a condition or disease which starts from the tips of twigs and moves down through the shoot. Any one of a number of fungal diseases, insects, climatic conditions, cultural practices, and soil chemistry can cause this symptom. Disease, however, should not be confused with a certain amount of "natural pruning," which takes place as the plant develops.

Verticillium wilt. This disease is one of the main causes of shoot or twig dieback in maples. Occasionally, the whole tree dies. At this stage, bluish-green to brown streaking can be seen in the sapwood when the branch is split. The tree may die in one year or over several years with branch after branch dying back. The spores of *Verticillium* wilt occur in the soil, and they enter the tree via damaged roots and root hairs. The first sign of trouble is the wilting of the leaves and dieback of young shoots. Wilt is widespread and can be serious. Meticulous sanitation during propagation, maintenance of plant vigor and health, and removal and burning of infected material help to limit further spread. If the tree dies, remove and burn all parts including as much of the root as possible. In the garden, it is a wise practice to clean pruning tools frequently with sterilants as a matter of routine, whether the disease is present or not.

Anthracnose (leaf blight). This fungus overwinters on dead shoots and attacks leaves the following spring, especially during wet cool conditions. It causes reddish-brown to purplish-brown spots to appear on the leaves, which become irregular dead patches. These spots may engulf entire young leaves, causing them to shrivel and die. The fungus then moves down the leafstalk into the shoot, eventually killing the infected shoot. By this stage there is no remedy.

Preventing anthracnose is more effective than curing it. Where an attack has occurred, all dead shoots should be pruned, removed, and burned, and preventative chemical sprays applied just before bud-break the following spring, then twice more 10–14 days apart. By this time, the leaves and shoots should have passed out of the vulnerable phase and, combined with warm weather, be strong enough to resist further attacks.

Leaf scorch. Whenever water is lost from the leaves faster than the roots can take it up, brown dead patches spread from the leaf tip and margin inwards between the veins. Defoliation and dieback of shoot tips follow prolonged droughts and heat. A wide range of environmental factors, such as drought, drying winds, and hot sun, can cause it. Salt-laden winds, excessive alkalinity or nitrogen in the soil, and spring frosts can all have similar effects. Leaf burning, caused by watering foliage during the sunniest and hottest part of the day, will have similar effects on many maple cultivars, especially the red dissectums.

Usually, the plant is not lost but appearance and vigor for at least that growing season are damaged. Watering and mulching can help to reduce the problem during drought and heat spells, but again prevention is better than cure. Plant maples in less-exposed conditions, partially sheltered from prevailing or cold winds and from afternoon sun in the hotter areas. The availability of water should be regular and consistent to avoid prolonged drying from whatever cause, and good mulching helps reduce moisture loss from the soil. Finally, in hot sunny conditions, water early or late in the day.

Chlorosis. This gradual or general yellowing of the leaves reflects a nutrient deficiency. It is most commonly associated with soils which are too acid or too alkaline, preventing the plants from taking up the nutrients concerned—normally one or a combination of essential micronutrients (trace elements). Remedies involving the application of proprietary iron solutions provide only temporary relief in high pH conditions. Hence, avoid planting maples in extremely acid or extremely alkaline conditions (such as in soils with pH below 5.6 or above 7.6). Instead, grow them in raised beds or containers.

JAPANESE MAPLES
FOR SPECIFIC PURPOSES AND LOCATIONS

The categories that follow are designed to suggest the qualities and uses of selected plants described in this volume. The lists are not comprehensive, and readers are encouraged to refer to the plant descriptions for information on a cultivar's suitability for a specific location or use.

Maples for Spring Color

'Akane' (yellow-orange)
'Ariadne' (pink-red variegation)
'Beni maiko' (red-pink)
'Beni shichihenge' (pink-red variegation)
'Beni tsukasa' (red-pink)
'Corallinum' (red-pink)
'Deshōjō' (red-pink)
'Higasa yama' (pink-red variegation)
'Katsura' (yellow-orange)
'Orange Dream' (yellow-orange)
'Shin deshōjō' (red)
'Ueno yama' (yellow-orange)
'Wilson's Pink Dwarf' (red-pink)

Maples for Fall Color

'Autumn Fire' (red)
'Hōgyoku' (orange)
'Ichigyōji' (yellow-orange)
'Inazuma' (red)
'Korean Gem' (yellow-orange)
'Nicholsonii' (yellow to red)
'Okushimo' (gold)
'Omure yama' (gold to crimson)
'Ōsakazuki' (crimson)
'Red Autumn Lace' (yellow to red)
'Seiryū' (gold to red)
'Shishigashira' (gold to red)
'Tobiosho' (red)
'Yezo nishiki' (crimson)

Maples for Winter Bark

'Aoyagi'
'Beni kawa'
'Fjellheim'
'Ibo nishiki'
'Japanese Sunrise'
'Nishiki gawa'
'Sango kaku'

Dwarf Maples
(to 6½ ft. [2 m] tall)

'Aratama' (green)
'Baby Lace' (green)
'Beni hime' (red)
'Brandt's Dwarf' (red)
'Coonara Pygmy' (green)
'Garyū' (green)
'Kamagata' (green)
'Kandy Kitchen' (red)
'Kashima' (green)
'Kiyo hime' (green)
'Koto ito komachi' (green)
'Mikawa yatsubusa' (green)
'Murasaki kiyohime' (green)
'Ōjishi' (green)
'Oto hime' (green)
'Pixie' (red)
'Ryūzu' (green)
'Seigen' (green)
'Sharp's Pygmy' (green)
'Shishio hime' (green)
'Tama hime' (green)
'Tsukomo' (green)
'Wilson's Pink Dwarf' (green)

Small Maples
(6½–13 ft. [2–4 m] tall)

'Ariadne' (variegated)
'Autumn Fire' (green)

Opposite: *Acer palmatum* and *Cedrus atlantica* 'Glauca'.
Photo by Peter Gregory.

'Beni ubi gohon' (red)
'Crimson Queen' (red)
'Ellen' (green)
'Felice' (red)
'Filigree' (variegated)
'Germaine's Gyration' (green)
'Goshiki shidare' (variegated)
'Hagoromo' (green)
'Kinshi' (green)
'Koshibori nishiki' (variegated)
'Lemon Lime Lace' (green)
'Maiko' (green)
'Nishiki gasane' (variegated)
'Orange Dream' (green)
'Orangeola' (red)
'Peaches and Cream' (variegated)
'Pink Filigree' (red)
'Red Pygmy' (red)
'Seigai' (green)
'Shaina' (red)
'Shigarami' (green)
'Shōjō' (red)
'Tsuchigumo' (green)
'Tsuma beni' (green)
'Ukigumo' (variegated)
'Villa Taranto' (green)
'Wabito' (green)

Medium-sized Maples (10–16 ft. [3–5 m] tall)

'Atrolineare' (red)
'Baldsmith' (red)
'Beni shi en' (variegated)
'Beni shigitatsu sawa' (variegated)
'Butterfly' (variegated)
'Chitose yama' (red)
'Dissectum Nigrum' (red)
'Garnet' (red)
'Kagerō' (variegated)
'Katsura' (green)
'Kinran' (red)
'Masu kagami' (variegated)
'Matsukaze' (green)
'Nanese gawa' (green)
'Octopus' (red)

'Omure yama' (green)
'Ornatum' (red)
'Ōshū shidare' (red)
'Palmatifidum' (green)
'Red Autumn Lace' (green)
'Rubrum' (red)
'Sherwood Flame' (red)
'Shigitatsu sawa' (variegated)
'Shin deshōjō' (green)
'Shinobuga oka' (green)
'Tsukushi gata' (red)
'Ueno yama' (green)
'Utsu semi' (green)

Large Maples (13–26 ft. [4–8 m] tall)

'Aoyagi' (green)
'Asahi zuru' (variegated)
'Beni ōtake' (red)
'Boskoop Glory' (red)
'Burgundy Lace' (red)
'Green Trompenburg' (green)
'Higasa yama' (variegated)
'Hōgyoku' (green)
'Kihachijō' (green)
'Korean Gem' (green)
'Nuresagi' (red)
'Oridono nishiki' (variegated)
'Sango kaku' (green)
'Seiryū' (green)
'Sumi nagashi' (red)
'Tana' (green)
'Yūbae' (variegated)

Very Large Maples (20 ft.+ [6 m+] tall)

'Attraction' (red)
'Bloodgood' (red)
'Iijima sunago' (variegated)
'Kogane nishiki' (green)
'Mirte' (green)
'Moonfire' (red)
'Ōsakazuki' (green)
'Shishigashira' (green)
'Versicolor' (variegated)

Maples for Partial Shade

These cultivars are not restricted to shade but are less likely to suffer sun scorch and exposure damage when grown in shade.
'Ariadne'
'Asahi zuru'
'Geisha'
'Goshiki shidare'
'Nishiki gasane'
'Orange Dream'
'Peaches and Cream'
'Seigen'
'Toyama nishiki'
'Tsuma beni'
'Ukigumo'

Maples for Full Sun

These cultivars benefit from full sun though some leaf tips may burn in extreme conditions. It is worth noting that the color of most red-leafed cultivars is more intense in full sun.
'Beni hime' (red)
'Boskoop Glory' (red)
'Japanese Sunrise' (green)
'Kamagata' (green)
'Kogane nishiki' (green)
'Pink Filigree' (red)
'Red Pygmy' (red)
'Seiryū' (green)

Maples for Containers

All *Acer palmatum* cultivars can be grown in containers. The restricted root growth helps limit the size of the larger plants.
'Beni hime' (red)
'Beni kumo-no-su' (red)
'Beni maiko' (red)
'Butterfly' (variegated)
'Kinran' (red)
'Kinshi' (green)
'Kiyo hime' (green)
'Shaina' (red)
'Shin deshōjō' (green)
'Shishigashira' (green)
'Shishio hime' (green)

Maples for the Rockery

'Aka kawa hime' (green)
'Alpenweiss' (variegated)
'Aratama' (red)
'Baby Lace' (green)
'Brandt's Dwarf' (red)
'Coonara Pygmy' (green)
'Garyū' (green)
'Kamagata' (green)
'Kandy Kitchen' (red)
'Seigen' (green)
'Sharp's Pygmy' (green)
'Wilson's Pink Dwarf' (green)

Maples for Bonsai

'Beni hime' (red)
'Beni ubi gohon' (red)
'Higasa yama' (variegated)
'Kiyo hime' (green)
'Murasaki kiyohime' (green)
'Oto hime' (green)
'Seigai' (green)
'Sekka yatsubusa' (green)
'Sharp's Pygmy' (green)
'Shin chishio' (green)
'Shin deshōjō' (green)
'Shishigashira' (green)
'Shishio hime' (green)

Dissectum Group

Maples with lacy leaves in which the very deeply divided leaf lobes are themselves deeply divided into sublobes.
'Autumn Fire' (green)
'Baldsmith' (red)
'Crimson Queen' (red)
'Dissectum Nigrum' (red)
'Ellen' (green)
'Emerald Lace' (green)
'Filigree' (variegated)
'Flavescens' (green)
'Garnet' (red)
'Germaine's Gyration' (green)
'Goshiki shidare' (variegated)
'Lemon Lime Lace' (green)

'Orangeola' (red)
'Ornatum' (red)
'Red Autumn Lace' (green)
'Red Filigree Lace' (red)
'Seiryū' (green)
'Sekimori' (green)
'Stella Rossa' (red)
'Toyama nishiki' (variegated)
'Waterfall' (green)

Amoenum Group

Maples with large leaves divided up to two-thirds of the way to the leaf base, and with finely toothed margins.
'Bloodgood' (red)
'Boskoop Glory' (red)
'Hōgyoku' (green)
'Ichigyōji' (green)
'Kagerō' (variegated)
'Korean Gem' (green)
'Ōsakazuki' (green)
'Rubrum' (red)
'Shōjō' (red)
'Tsukuba ne' (green)
'Tsukushi gata' (red)
'Tsuma beni' (green)
'Utsu semi' (green)
'Yūbae' (variegated)

Palmatum Group

Maples with small leaves usually divided more than two-thirds of the way to the leaf base, and with coarsely toothed margins.
'Aoyagi' (green)
'Asahi zuru' (variegated)
'Beni komachi' (red)
'Beni maiko' (red)
'Butterfly' (variegated)
'Corallinum' (red)
'Eddisbury' (green)
'Japanese Sunrise' (green)
'Kasen nishiki' (variegated)
'Katsura' (green)
'Maiko' (green)
'Ō kagami' (red)
'Orange Dream' (green)
'Oridono nishiki' (variegated)

'Otome zakura' (red)
'Sagara nishiki' (variegated)
'Sango kaku' (green)
'Shaina' (red)
'Shin chishio' (green)
'Shishigashira' (green)
'Tsuchigumo' (green)

Matsumurae Group

Maples with large leaves deeply divided to more than three-fourths of the way to the leaf base, and with coarsely toothed margins.
'Ariadne' (variegated)
'Azuma murasaki' (red)
'Beni shigitatsu sawa' (variegated)
'Burgundy Lace' (red)
'Chitose yama' (red)
'Elegans' (green)
'Green Trompenburg' (green)
'Higasa yama' (variegated)
'Iijima sunago' (variegated)
'Kihachijō' (green)
'Matsukaze' (green)
'Moonfire' (red)
'Nuresagi' (red)
'Omure yama' (green)
'Peaches and Cream' (variegated)
'Purple Ghost' (variegated)
'Shigitatsu sawa' (variegated)
'Shigure bato' (green)
'Shinonome' (green)
'Sumi nagashi' (red)
'Trompenburg' (red)
'Wakehurst Pink' (variegated)
'Yasemin' (red)

Linearilobum Group

Maples with very narrow, straplike leaf lobes.
'Atrolineare' (red)
'Beni ōtake' (red)
'Beni ubi gohon' (red)
'Fairy Hair' (green)
'Kinshi' (green)
'Red Pygmy' (red)
'Shinobuga oka' (green)
'Villa Taranto' (green)

Maples with a Wide-spreading Habit

'Ariadne' (variegated)
'Beni kagami' (red)
'Beni shigitatsu sawa' (variegated)
'Hessei' (red)
'Japanese Sunrise' (green)
'Nanese gawa' (green)
'Sazanami' (green)
'Tsukushi gata' (red)
'Yezo nishiki' (red)

Maples with a Rounded Habit

'Asahi zuru' (variegated)
'Deshōjō' (red)
'Hōgyoku' (green)
'Ichigyōji' (green)
'Iijima sunago' (variegated)
'Inazuma' (red)
'Kihachijō' (green)
'Kinran' (red)
'Korean Gem' (green)
'Moonfire' (red)
'Musashino' (red)
'Oridono nishiki' (variegated)
'Ōsakazuki' (green)
'Red Pygmy' (red)
'Sherwood Flame' (red)
'Tsuma beni' (green)
'Tsuma gaki' (green)
'Villa Taranto' (green)
'Wakehurst Pink' (variegated)

Mound-shaped Maples

It is worth noting that, in addition to the cultivars listed below, almost all dissectums are mound-shaped.

'Chitose yama' (red)
'Koshibori nishiki' (variegated)
'Matsukaze' (green)
'Omure yama' (green)
'Ōshū shidare' (red)
'Peaches and Cream' (red)

Upright Maples

'Aoyagi' (green)
'Atrolineare' (red)
'Beni shichihenge' (variegated)
'Bloodgood' (red)
'Burgundy Lace' (red)
'Butterfly' (variegated)
'Green Trompenburg' (green)
'Higasa yama' (variegated)
'Katsura' (green)
'Ō kagami' (red)
'Okushimo' (green)
'Orange Dream' (green)
'Oshio beni' (red)
'Sango kaku' (green)
'Shigitatsu sawa' (variegated)
'Shishigashira' (green)
'Trompenburg' (red)
'Ueno yama' (green)
'Versicolor' (variegated)
'Whitney Red' (red)
'Yasemin' (red)

ACER PALMATUM AND ITS CULTIVARS

Most Japanese maple cultivars belong to *Acer palmatum*, commonly known as smooth Japanese maple because of the texture of its bark. Three subspecies are currently recognized: subsp. *palmatum*, subsp. *amoenum*, and subsp. *matsumurae*.

Subsp. *palmatum* has small green leaves, with five to seven lobes palmately arranged, hence the name. These are usually divided more than halfway, sometimes almost entirely, to the leaf base. The lobes are ovate to long-ovate, ending in a sharp tip, and have coarsely toothed margins. The small red-and-cream flowers appear in late spring or early summer and develop into small winged fruit (called *samaras*), ripening in early or midautumn. This subspecies forms an upright tree, usually with a domed or broad canopy. In its natural habit, the tree reaches a height of 49 ft. (15 m). It is hardy and adapts to a wide range of growing and climatic conditions. Subspecies *palmatum* is confined to Japan and southwestern Korea, where it grows in moist valleys and along streamsides up to an elevation of 3630 ft. (1100 m).

Subsp. *amoenum* has larger, usually seven-lobed leaves divided up to two-thirds of the way to the leaf base. The leaf margins are evenly and finely toothed. The flowers and fruits are much larger than those of subsp. *palmatum*. Subsp. *amoenum* is found as an understory tree in and on the edge of mountain forests throughout Japan, and in southwestern coastal areas of China and Korea.

Subsp. *matsumurae*, like subsp. *amoenum*, has larger leaves, flowers, and fruits, but the seven- to nine-lobed leaves are usually very deeply divided, sometimes completely, to the leaf base and have coarsely toothed margins. This subspecies is the most shrublike and, if it forms a small tree, it rarely exceeds 26–30 ft. (8–9 m) high. It is native to Japan in mountain forests at elevations up to 4300 ft. (1300 m), as part of the understory.

For ease of comparison and recognition, the numerous cultivars of *Acer palmatum* are divided into seven groups, based mainly on the characteristics of the subspecies and on the depth of the division of the leaf lobes or, in the case of the dwarf group, the mature height of the cultivar. These groups are as follows:

1. **Palmatum Group:** Small leaves with coarsely toothed margins and moderately to deeply divided lobes.

2. **Amoenum Group:** Large leaves with finely toothed margins and shallowly to moderately deeply divided lobes.

3. **Matsumurae Group:** Large leaves with coarsely toothed margins and moderately deeply to very deeply divided lobes.

4. **Linearilobum Group:** Leaf lobes narrow, straplike, divided almost to the leaf base. Also known as the strapleaves.

5. **Dissectum Group:** Leaf lobes very deeply divided and deeply dissected into sublobes. Also known as the laceleaves.

The five basic leaf shapes of *Acer palmatum* (clockwise from bottom left): 1 and 2, Palmatum Group; 3, Linearilobum Group; 4, Amoenum Group; 5, Dissectum Group; 6, Matsumurae Group. Photo by Andrea Jones.

Opposite: *Acer palmatum* cultivars in a woodland setting at Westonbirt Arboretum, Gloucestershire, England. Photo by Peter Gregory.

6. **Dwarf Group**: Cultivars whose mature height does not usually exceed 6½ ft. (2 m).

7. **Other Group**: Cultivars that cannot be placed in any of the above groups.

'Aka kawa hime'

Palmatum Group—green. This outstanding semi-dwarf form of the popular 'Sango kaku' retains all the desirable attributes of its parent—fresh yellow-green spring foliage, bright red shoots and leafstalks, eye-catching yellow, gold, and red fall colors, and attractive coral-red winter stems. The leaves of these two cultivars are identical in shape, size, and seasonal coloring, but 'Aka kawa hime' is unlikely to exceed 6–10 ft. (1.8–3 m) in height, making it ideal for container culture and small gardens. The name means "small red bark."

'Akane'

Palmatum Group—green. The bright orange-yellow spring leaves with deep pink margins con-trast well with the coral-red leafstalks and shoots. The spring colors last for almost a month, then turn a deep, clear yellow, gradually becoming light green. The fall color is orange to yellow with red blushing. The small moderately to deeply divided five-lobed leaves are usually longer than broad. The lobes are ovate-triangular with pointed tips and clearly toothed margins. The short, slender leafstalks are red. Slow growing, this delightful compact semidwarf tree is unlikely to exceed 10 ft. (3 m) at maturity, with a spread of about 5 ft. (1.5 m). The name means "glowing evening sky," which describes perfectly the spring color of the leaves.

'Akegarasu'

Amoenum Group—red. The large leaves are very deeply divided into five to seven broadly ovate-elliptic lobes, with very sharp tips and toothed margins. The early season color is a very deep purple-red becoming bronze-green in the summer.

Acer palmatum 'Aka kawa hime'. Photo by Francis Schroeder.

Acer palmatum 'Akane'. Photo by Cor van Gelderen.

Acer palmatum 'Akegarasu'. Photo by Peter Gregory.

Like other reds, when grown in shady conditions it has a less intense color. The leafstalks are deep red and the branches green. This strong, upright-growing maple reaches at least 16 ft. (5 m) at maturity. It tends to widen into a broad-topped, short tree. It is both hardy and easy to grow. The name means "the crows at dawn."

'Alpenweiss'

Palmatum Group—variegated. This maple is very similar to but smaller than the outstanding old Japanese cultivar 'Higasa yama' and is thought to be even more colorful as the buds open in the spring. The small five-lobed leaves are deeply divided and about the same size and shape as those of the popular variegate 'Butterfly'. 'Alpenweiss' forms a vase-shaped tree and is estimated to grow to 10 ft. (3 m) tall with a spread of about 4 ft. (1.3 m) in approximately 10 years. It is ideal for small gardens and container culture. The name means "white alpine."

'Amber Ghost'

Matsumurae Group—variegated. The spring leaves are a delightful amber with a network of dark veins, the colors becoming darker through the summer. The large, deeply divided leaves have five to seven ovate lobes with long-pointed tips and fairly evenly toothed but slightly crumpled margins. This cultivar from Oregon forms a semi-upright tree to about 13 ft. (4 m) tall and 8 ft. (2.5 m) wide. It adds another attractive color to the garden landscape.

'Ao kanzashi'

Palmatum Group—variegated. An upright, densely branched, small to medium-sized tree or shrub, 'Ao kanzashi' attains up to 13 ft. (4 m) tall and has a crown that spreads out at the top like 'Butterfly'. The small, deeply divided blue-green leaves have sporadically colored margins. 'Ao kanzashi' is very like 'Tennyo-no-hoshi' in leaf shape, variegation, and habit, but has slightly

Acer palmatum 'Alpenweiss'. Photo by Cor van Gelderen.

Acer palmatum 'Amber Ghost'. Photo by Talon Buchholz.

Acer palmatum 'Ao kanzashi'. Photo by Peter Gregory.

smaller leaves and more compact growth. The light cream-green variegation around the leaf edges does not turn pink in the sun as readily as does that of 'Tennyo-no-hoshi'. The name means "blue-green margins," referring to the leaves.

'Aoba jō'

Dwarf Group—green. This strong-growing dwarf shrub has medium-sized, moderately deeply divided seven-lobed leaves that are broader than long. The bases are flat and the lobes are ovate-lanceolate with long, tapering points and notched margins. The leaf color is strong green with bronzed edges and tips, becoming yellow with reddish hues in the fall. This cultivar is popular with bonsai enthusiasts and attractive in the right place as a dwarf in the landscape. The name means "beautiful green leaves."

'Aoyagi'

Palmatum Group—green. The bright pea-green color of the bark on twigs and limbs is the out-standing feature of this cultivar, which is sometimes referred to as the green counterpart of 'Sango kaku'. The small green leaves have five to seven moderately deeply divided lobes which radiate outwards and taper gradually to long, sharp points. The margins are toothed. The bright green is of a light tone and becomes a pleasing yellow in the fall. Upright-growing, this wide-topped tree reaches 20–26 ft. (6–8 m) tall as it matures but is not as vigorous as 'Sango kaku'. When planted near the contrasting 'Sango kaku', the effect is pleasing. The beauty of the stem color is enhanced by snow. The name means "green coral." Synonym, 'Ukon'.

'Volubile' is similar to 'Aoyagi' in leaf shape, size, and early season color, without the beautiful green twigs.

'Arakawa'

Palmatum Group—green. Selected for its corky bark, this cultivar begins to produce roughly textured bark when it is three to five years old and

Acer palmatum 'Aoba jō'. Photo by Cor van Gelderen.

Acer palmatum 'Aoyagi'. Photo by Cor van Gelderen.

develops rapidly each year, though it does not become as deeply fissured as 'Nishiki gawa'. The small green leaves have five to seven moderately deeply divided, narrowly ovate lobes which taper gradually to long, slender points and radiate outwards. The margins are double-toothed. Fall color is yellow-gold. The red leafstalks are short and slender. This vigorous, upright plant matures at more than 26 ft. (8 m) tall. It can be used for bonsai and makes a very interesting plant. The rough bark is prominent even when the plant is dwarfed. The name means "rough bark."

Acer palmatum 'Arakawa'. Photo by Robert Jamgochian.

'Aratama'

Dwarf Group—red. This highly desirable dwarf shrub has small bright red foliage varying from brick-red in the older leaves to light purple-red in the new leaves. During the summer a green tinge often appears along the midribs, giving an interesting two-tone effect. The five to seven leaf lobes are long-ovate with long, tapering points and well-toothed margins. The moderately deeply divided leaves have flat bases, and the center lobes are often shortened. Originating as a witches' broom of 'Koi murasaki', this cultivar forms a round, dense, twiggy, shrubby plant with the leaves lying rather flat along the twigs. It reaches 3–5 ft. (1–1.5 m) tall in 10 years and is suitable for the small garden landscape. It takes full sun very well. The name means "uncut gem."

Acer palmatum 'Aratama'. Photo by Peter Gregory.

'Ariadne'

Matsumurae Group—variegated. Like other members of the 'Shigitatsu sawa' group of cultivars, 'Ariadne' has marbled leaves in contrasting colors to the network of veins. New growth is especially attractive with yellow-green veining on a light orange-pink-red marbled background. Leaf color gradually changes to become red-veined on a purplish-red background by late summer. In the fall, the veins are yellow-green on an orange-pink-red marbled background with a deeper pink-red spreading inward from the margins. This cultivar also has attractive green young stems with fine, closely packed glaucous striations and lovely red fruits. The large five- to seven-lobed leaves are very deeply cut. The narrowly ovate lobes have tail-like tips and coarsely, sharply pointed toothed margins. 'Ariadne' matures to a shrub 10 ft. (3 m) tall and at least as wide. The name honors a granddaughter of D. M. van Gelderen, whose nursery introduced this plant.

Acer palmatum 'Ariadne'. Photo by Peter Gregory.

'Ariake nomura'

Amoenum Group—red. This seedling of 'Musashino' has leaves identical in size and shape but a browner-red spring color, lighter purplish-red-bronze in late summer, and a bright crimson in the fall. 'Ariake nomura' forms a medium-sized

Acer palmatum 'Ariake nomura'. Photo by Peter Gregory.

upright tree and is thought by some to be more graceful than its parent. The name means "beautiful dawn."

'Asahi zuru'

Palmatum Group—variegated. An old dependable cultivar, 'Asahi zuru' is known for its sharply defined clear white variegation on a rich green background. The leaves vary considerably in markings. Some are almost entirely white, while others are almost completely green. The variegated patches on the spring growth are a light pink before becoming white. The small five-lobed leaves are usually symmetrical, but some have sickle-shaped lobes when containing white sections. Twigs and small branches are dark green and do not have the pink striping often present in the similar 'Oridono nishiki'. This upright but spreading, round-headed tree can reach 26 ft. (8 m) high and 10–13 ft. (3–4 m) wide. It is desirable in many landscape situations. Afternoon shade helps prevent excessive leaf burn. The name means "the dawn swan."

'Atrolineare'

Linearilobum Group—red. In its prime in the early season, the stringlike foliage is dark red, bronzing out with greenish undertones. The leaf has five to seven widely separated, very narrow lobes which are divided completely to the base. The midrib of each lobe is green. This upright-growing small form reaches a height of 13 ft. (4 m) and is very desirable in contrast to the more round-headed strap-leaved cultivars, such as 'Red Pygmy' and 'Villa Taranto'. Synonym, 'Linearilobum Atropurpureum'. The name refers to the very dark-colored, narrow leaves.

'Attraction'

Palmatum Group—red. The large five- to seven-lobed leaves of this Japanese cultivar are deeply divided. The lobes are long-ovate, gradually tapering to a sharp point, and have regularly toothed margins. The short, stiff leafstalks are red. The leaves are a deep purple-red to maroon, brightest on new leaves, becoming deeper with maturity, but not as deep as 'Bloodgood' or as

Acer palmatum 'Asahi zuru'. Photo by Cor van Gelderen.

Acer palmatum 'Atrolineare'. Photo by Harold Greer.

Acer palmatum 'Attraction'. Photo by Harold Greer.

Acer palmatum 'Aureum'. Photo by J. D. Vertrees.

resistant to sunburn. The leaves turn a striking bright crimson in the fall. This perfectly hardy cultivar becomes a tall upright round-headed tree up to 23 ft. (7 m) tall. Synonym, 'Superbum'.

'Aureum'

Palmatum Group—green. The distinctive golden-yellow leaves are quite striking in the spring, with a slight rust-pink tinge on the leaf margins. The margin color soon disappears and, as the season progresses, the leaves become a light green, the "golden" tone softening. In full sun, the yellow color develops into the golden shades. Fall color is bright yellow. The medium-sized leaves have five to seven lobes and are almost circular. The margins are slightly toothed. The short leafstalks and the shoots are bright red. This upright, bushy tree reaches up to 26 ft. (8 m) at maturity. The name means "golden-yellow."

'Autumn Fire'

Dissectum Group—green. The form of this cultivar differs from that of most dissectums in being semierect rather than dome-shaped. The outstanding feature is the medium green leaves that turn an intense brilliant red in the fall. New growth is a light yellow-green with pink edging and makes an attractive contrast with the darker green older foliage. The large, very coarse leaves are deeply divided into seven to nine lobes and have surprisingly small, narrow, sharply pointed teeth. The lobes themselves are not as deeply divided as are those of most laceleafs. 'Autumn Fire' forms a vigorous, semierect, wide-spreading bush, reaching only about 6½ ft. (2 m) high in 10 years, but spreading even wider.

'Autumn Glory'

Matsumurae Group—green. This Belgium cultivar is noted for its beautiful fall color display. The

Acer palmatum 'Autumn Fire'. Photo by Harold Greer.

Acer palmatum 'Autumn Glory'. Photo by Peter Gregory.

typical, medium-sized leaves are deeply divided into five to seven lobes with coarsely toothed margins. Spring leaves are yellow-green with pink-red tinged margins, soon becoming medium green for summer, then turning brilliant crimson in the fall. 'Autumn Glory' forms a small broad upright-growing tree up to 20 ft. (6 m) tall.

'Azuma murasaki'

Matsumurae Group—red. Distinguishing this cultivar are the deeply divided purplish-red leaves with an undertone of green showing through. New foliage is a yellow-orange color with a fine pubescent covering which soon disappears. In the summer, the red leaves develop a deep green tinge. The medium-sized leaves are divided into seven lobes. Each lobe separates widely from the rest, is long, ovate-lanceolate, and has toothed margins. The leafstalks are bright red. 'Azuma murasaki' reaches 20 ft. (6 m) high, becoming round-topped and about 16 ft. (5 m) wide. Outside shoots take on a cascading form in time. The color of this choice tree is different enough to make a good contrast in the garden landscape. The name means "purple of the East."

'Baby Lace'

Dwarf Group—green. Highly desirable, 'Baby Lace' is the first dissectum witches' broom to be discovered. The finely dissected leaves are half the size of normal dissectum leaves in the first year, becoming smaller with age until reduced to the size of a thumbnail. The leaves emerge a reddish orange in the spring, becoming bronze-green for the summer, and turning orange-red to pink-red in the fall. During the summer, the orange-red new growth is an attractive color contrast to the darker bronze-green mature leaves. 'Baby Lace' reaches about 3 ft. (1 m) tall and wide after 10 years and eventually forms a small round, densely twigged shrub. It is very sensitive to wind and needs protection for at least the first three to four years.

'Baldsmith'

Dissectum Group—red. The light, bright orange-red spring foliage becomes green-tinged in the center with pink-tinged margins as the leaves develop. The combination of mature and new leaves through the summer gives a multicolored appearance of greens, pinks, and orange-reds,

Acer palmatum 'Azuma murasaki'. Photo by J. D. Vertrees.

Acer palmatum 'Baby Lace'. Photo by Harold Greer.

Acer palmatum 'Baldsmith'. Photo by Harry Olsen.

Acer palmatum 'Barrie Bergman'. Photo by Peter Gregory.

Acer palmatum 'Beni chidori'. Photo by Cor van Gelderen.

Acer palmatum 'Beni gasa'. Photo by Peter Gregory.

turning a bright yellow with orange hues in the fall. The medium-sized five- to seven-lobed leaves are finely dissected. 'Baldsmith' has the usual mounded habit and vigor of most dissectums but finely dissected light orange-red foliage, which contrasts sharply with the deeper reds of 'Crimson Queen' and 'Dissectum Nigrum'.

'Barrie Bergman'

Dissectum Group—red. Slow-growing and compact, 'Barrier Bergman' has finely dissected leaves. The bright pink-red new growth makes an attractive contrast to the purple-red to bronze-red older leaves. Bronze-green tones readily appear on plants growing in partial shade. Fall color is orange-red. This cultivar forms a dense mound-shaped plant which is surprisingly hardy.

'Beni chidori'

Palmatum Group—green. This Japanese cultivar is one of the bright pink-red spring color maples, similar to the popular 'Corallinum'. The new leaves emerge a deep pink-red, changing to orange-red with yellow veins and margins, and becoming medium green for the summer. Fall color is scarlet. The shoots and leafstalks are red. The small five- to seven-lobed leaves are moderately deeply divided. 'Beni chidori' grows slowly to about 10 ft. (3 m) tall and is ideal for bonsai and container growing. The name means "red plover."

'Beni gasa'

Matsumurae Group—red. This American cultivar has medium-sized five- to seven-lobed fan-shaped leaves. The lobes are deeply divided with conspicuous coarse, sharp teeth on the crinkled margins. The new leaves are a bright pink-red, with contrasting lime-green midveins and stalks, becoming dark brown-red to purple-red for the summer. Fall color is an attractive blend of gold and crimson. This slow-growing broad shrubby tree makes a welcome addition to the garden landscape. The name means "red umbrella."

'Beni hime'

Dwarf Group—red. Among the smallest red dwarf shrubs, 'Beni hime' has tiny, fine-pointed, star-shaped leaves with short acuminate, moderately deeply divided lobes. The leaves are clustered on short leafstalks, forming a dense compact bush. Full sun deepens the red color which becomes green-tinged by midsummer. Fall color is a vibrant red. Although it tends to show mold damage on new growth, this maple is hardy in open situations with plenty of light, which discourages the mold. It attains a height and width of 3 ft. (1 m) in 8–10 years and is ideally suited to container culture and bonsai. The name means "red dwarf."

Acer palmatum 'Beni hime'. Photo by Peter Gregory.

'Beni hoshi'

Dwarf Group—green. The leaves are bright red in the spring, turning green during the summer. A second growth of new leaves creates splashes of red on a green background, which persists until the leaves turn yellow to orange in the fall. The small seven-lobed wide-spreading palmate leaves are moderately deeply divided. Each broad lobe tapers to a short tail-like tip and has fine-toothed margins. The leafstalks are short and stiff. 'Beni hoshi' forms a compact dwarf tree, reaching 6 ft. (1.8 m) high in 15 years. It is suitable for the small garden, container culture, and bonsai. The name means "red star."

Acer palmatum 'Beni hoshi'. Photo Harold Greer.

'Ruby Star' appears to be identical to 'Beni hoshi'.

'Beni kagami'

Matsumurae Group—red. In the spring, the medium-sized leaves are orange-red to purplish red. Fall color is a bright crimson. The palmate leaves are very deeply divided into seven long, narrowly ovate lobes and have toothed margins. The short leafstalks are bright red. This fairly strong grower forms a spreading medium-sized tree and reaches a height of 26 ft. (8 m) at maturity. The form is quite graceful. The name means "red mirror."

Acer palmatum 'Beni kagami'. Photo by J. D. Vertrees.

Acer palmatum 'Beni komachi'. Photo by Harold Greer.

'Beni komachi'

Palmatum Group—red. This semidwarf cultivar has unusual leaves of brilliant red. Each small leaf has five lobes that are separated almost entirely to the base. The lobes extend widely and openly, the basal two extending obliquely backward. Each lobe is long, narrows to a sharp tip, and curls sideways and/or down. The lobe sides may bend slightly upwards to form a shallow trough. The margins are irregularly but markedly toothed. The new foliage is a bright crimson which then darkens before becoming greenish red in the summer with the margins remaining crimson. Fall color is scarlet. 'Beni komachi' forms a small bush up to 10 ft. (3 m) tall. The name means "beautiful red-haired little girl."

'Beni fushigi' is similar to 'Beni komachi' but easier to grow, with deeper bright red foliage and not as small at maturity.

'Beni kumo-no-su'

Dissectum Group—red. The seven-lobed leaves are bright red in the spring, gradually changing to bronze-red in the summer, later becoming bronze-green before turning bright red in the fall. The red leafstalks are short and slender. This cultivar forms a low, dense, broad bush with outwardly spreading pendulous branches. It reaches up to 8 ft. (2.5 m) tall but spreads even wider. It has one of the smallest and finest cut leaves of any dissectum, and is ideal for the small garden, rock garden, patio, or container culture. The name means "red spider's web."

'Beni maiko'

Palmatum Group—red. The fire-red or scarlet leaves of spring become greenish red in the summer, with the main veins and leafstalks remaining red. Fall color is a fiery red. The small leaves are

Acer palmatum 'Beni kumo-no-su'. Photo by Harry Olsen.

Acer palmatum 'Beni maiko'. Photo by Peter Gregory.

five-lobed, irregular, and slightly wrinkled. The lobes, with blunt tips and toothed margins, are divided halfway to the leaf base and tend to curve sideways. The leafstalks are very short. 'Beni maiko' forms a compact shrub up to 10 ft. (3 m) tall and is striking with its spring color. It is very adaptable to container culture. The name means "red-haired dancing girl."

'Beni ōtake'

Linearilobum Group—red. This attractive, vigorous upright cultivar has a distinctive bamboolike appearance and shape. The deep purple-red foliage is outstanding in the spring, the red color holding throughout summer, changing to vivid crimson in the fall. The large five- to seven-lobed leaves are widely spread. Each straplike lobe is broader than the lobes of most linearilobums, with long tail-like pointed tips and sharply

Acer palmatum 'Beni ōtake'. Photo by Peter Gregory.

pointed teeth along most margins. 'Beni ōtake' may reach 26 ft. (8 m) high at maturity. The name means "big red bamboo."

'Beni shi en'

Palmatum Group—variegated. The almost strap-like deeply divided leaves of this unusual cultivar change color throughout the growing season but hold their color well in full sun. The young feathery leaves emerge a rosy red, changing to purple and then medium green with conspicuous light green midribs. Many lobes develop light green edging, often causing the lobes to become sickle-shaped. The leaves take on a pinkish hue in late summer and turn golden in the fall. The very deeply divided medium-sized leaves have five to seven long, narrow oblong-ovate lobes with long tail-like tips and coarse teeth. Occasionally, some leaves are distorted. The green leafstalks are short and slender. 'Beni

shi en' is moderately vigorous and forms a small upright tree reaching about 18 ft. (5.5 m) at maturity. It makes an excellent small specimen in the landscape, with changing seasonal interest. The name means "red smoke."

'Beni shichihenge'

Palmatum Group—variegated. The outstanding feature is the variegated leaf coloration, similar to 'Kagiri nishiki' and 'Butterfly', but with pink-orange markings in the spring rather than pink. Basic leaf color is green or bluish green, with strong white margins. The white is overlaid or blushed with pink-orange, which becomes orange-brown later in the summer. Occasionally, the entire lobe is orange. Each five- to seven-lobed leaf varies in size and shape. Some lobes are very slender and uniform, while others are contorted and of different widths. The short leaf-stalks are crimson. 'Beni shichihenge' is slow

Acer palmatum 'Beni shigitatsu sawa'. Photo by Peter Gregory.

Acer palmatum 'Beni shichihenge'. Photo by Daniel Otis.

growing and forms an upright shrub up to 16 ft. (5 m) tall, with a spread of 6½ ft. (2 m). It is highly desirable and attracts much attention, especially in the spring. The name means "red and changeful."

'Beni shigitatsu sawa'

Matsumurae Group—variegated. This red-tinged form of 'Shigitatsu sawa' has more deeply divided narrower seven-lobed leaves. The leaf edges are wavy, irregularly curved downwards, and edged with sharp coarse teeth. The striking feature is the strong pink- and red-marbled overtones on the green background. 'Beni shigitatsu sawa' becomes a bushy plant up to 13 ft. (4 m) tall and slightly wider. Although not as strong-growing as its green counterpart, it makes a very interesting specimen plant. The name means "red snipe flying up from a winter swamp." Synonym, 'Aka shigitatsu sawa'.

'Beni tsukasa'

Palmatum Group—red. In the spring, the small leaves are an eye-catching bright orange-red or peach tone, changing to delicate shades of pink and red with greenish undertones, often showing strong yellow-green veins, and turning to green with lighter mottling in early summer before becoming a uniform medium green. The small leaves have five to seven ovate-lanceolate moderately deeply divided lobes, each tapering to a slender tip and with toothed margins. This willowy, slender-twigged plant makes a medium-sized tree up to 16 ft. (5 m) tall but usually smaller. It is a fine accent plant in small garden landscapes and lends itself to container culture. The name might be interpreted as meaning "the red master."

Acer palmatum 'Beni tsukasa'. Photo by J. D. Vertrees.

'Beni ubi gohon'

Linearilobum Group—red. The smallest strapleaf, both in leaf dimensions and ultimate size, this unique cultivar attains a little more than 6½ ft. (2 m) high. The small five-lobed straplike leaves have basal lobes held at right angles or pointing slightly forward. Each lobe has a sharp-pointed tip and fine-toothed margins. The red leafstalks are slender and short. The spring leaf color is a light bronze-red with green-tinged bases, rapidly becoming purple-red, which holds well throughout the summer in full sun. This cultivar makes an unusual and attractive container plant and may be well suited to bonsai culture. The name means "fine long red fingers," referring to the straplike leaves.

'Beni zuru'

Palmatum Group—green. The orange-yellow spring foliage is similar to that of 'Akane'. The small green leaves have mainly five long-ovate deeply divided lobes with coarsely toothed margins. In the spring, the leaves emerge a bright orange-pink-red with yellow midribs, changing slowly from the center to orange-yellow, then yellow, and finally light green for the rest of the summer, and eventually turning red in the fall. This small cultivar is ideally suited for container and bonsai culture. The name means "red swan."

'Berrima Bridge'

Dissectum Group—green. The main feature of this Australian cultivar is the unusual sequence of color changes throughout the growing season. The leaves emerge green in the spring and slowly become reddish green, then bronze-green through the summer, turning fiery red in the fall. 'Berrima Bridge' grows vigorously in the early years, eventually forming a domed mound 8–13 ft. (2.5–4 m) tall. The name honors the nursery which introduced this plant.

Acer palmatum 'Beni ubi gohon'. Photo by Harry Olsen.

Acer palmatum 'Beni zuru'. Photo by Peter Gregory.

Acer palmatum 'Berrima Bridge'. Photo by Cor van Gelderen.

Acer palmatum 'Berry Dwarf'. Photo by Francis Schroeder.

'Berry Dwarf'

Dwarf Group—green. The attractive distinctly shaped, relatively large bronze-green leaves are held on olive-green leafstalks and shoots. Spring leaves are a light apple-green, becoming tinged with orange before turning a rusty bronze-green for the summer. The unusually large (for a dwarf) five-lobed leaves spread outward like stars. Each lobe is broadly ovate with a pointed tip. There are about three pairs of irregular lobules along the lobe margins which themselves are coarsely toothed. Some leaves display the characteristic witches'-broom stubby central lobe. 'Berry Dwarf' forms a wide-spreading, dense, twiggy, low bush with a spread of 10 ft. (3 m) in 10 years but a height of only 3 ft. (1 m). It makes a very good groundcover

plant and was named after the Australian city in which the nursery that introduced it is located.

'Bewley's Red'

Dissectum Group—red. This Australian introduction is notable because of its unusual upright rounded growth habit, in contrast to the typical mushroom shape of most dissectums. It is slow growing, eventually reaching 10 ft. (3 m) tall, and is at its best in full sun.

'Bloodgood'

Palmatum—red. Among the most popular large-leaved, upright cultivars, 'Bloodgood' is the standard by which all other red cultivars are judged. It is a very good deep red or black-red and holds its

Acer palmatum 'Bewley's Red'. Photo by Peter Gregory.

Acer palmatum 'Bloodgood'. Photo by J. D. Vertrees.

Acer palmatum 'Boskoop Glory'. Photo by Cor van Gelderen.

Acer palmatum 'Brandt's Dwarf'. Photo by Harry Olsen.

Acer palmatum 'Burgundy Lace'. Photo by Cor van Gelderen.

color into late summer. The lobes are deeply divided. Fall color is bright crimson. The dark red leafstalks and prominent bright red fruits add to the attraction of the plant. This strong-growing cultivar makes a broad-topped tree maturing at up to 33 ft. (10 m) tall.

'Emperor I', an outstanding red cultivar of exceptional vigor, is comparable to 'Bloodgood' but comes into leaf two weeks later, thus reducing the risk of damage by late spring frosts and cold drying winds. It holds its color well in shade and is more versatile. 'Red Emperor' also fits this description and originates from the same nursery, hence may be the same cultivar.

'Fireglow' also is similar to 'Bloodgood', but the leaves are not as deeply divided. It has a deeper, more intense deep red color which stays throughout the summer. 'Fireglow' forms an upright shrub with many slender dark red shoots, eventually reaching up to 13–16 ft. (4–5 m) high. It makes an excellent garden or container plant.

'Boskoop Glory'

Amoenum Group—red. This dependable, robust, vigorous large tree has large, deep red leaves which hold their color well throughout the summer. The ultimate height is 20–26 ft. (6–8 m). The large five- to seven-lobed leaves are moderately deeply divided with numerous sharp fine teeth on the margins. The short stout leafstalks are also red. New leaves emerge a bright pink-red, changing to deep plum-red in the summer then gradually becoming purple-red with green undertones. This tree tolerates full sun very well. The name honors the town in the Netherlands where the nursery is located that introduced this plant.

'Brandt's Dwarf'

Dwarf Group—red. One of the best-known and oldest witches' brooms, 'Brandt's Dwarf' produces bright plum-red foliage in the spring, quickly changing to a good dark red, then slowly fading to a rusty green later in the season. It turns a brilliant crimson in the fall. The small leaves are deeply divided into five to seven lobes which are well spread outward. Each lobe is ovate with a long, tapering tip and finely toothed margins. The center lobe often has a short rounded top. At maturity this cultivar forms a dense rounded bush up to about 3 ft. (1 m) tall and wide.

'Burgundy Lace'

Matsumurae Group—red. This striking American cultivar has almost ribbonlike lobes colored burgundy wine. The medium-sized leaves are very deeply divided into seven ovate-lanceolate lobes. Each lobe narrows to a long, sharp tip and is

Acer palmatum 'Butterfly'. Photo by Peter Gregory.

edged with sharp teeth. Spring and early summer color is burgundy red, turning bronze-green later. The leaves burn in full sun. This spreading, small tree, up to 20 ft. (6 m) high and wide, develops a wide canopy. It is hardy and beautiful and makes an excellent contrast with other upright cultivars.

'Butterfly'

Palmatum Group—variegated. The small five-lobed leaves of this spectacular Japanese cultivar are borne on short leafstalks and vary in shape; rarely are any two alike. The long, slender lobes are separated almost to the leaf base. The leaf variegation, mainly around the margins, is basically a cream or whitish color on a bluish-green to grayish-green or pale green. Often the cream portion of the lobe is sickle-shaped. In the fall, the white areas become a striking magenta. This cultivar forms a small upright tree 16–20 ft. (5–6 m) high. It is one of the most reliable and desirable members of the variegated group.

'Carlis Corner'

Dwarf Group—red. Originating from a witches' broom in New Jersey, this attractive dwarf cultivar has very small palmate leaves, similar to those of 'Tiny Tim'. The leaves emerge a bright pink-red, changing to a rich purple-red and holding this color well throughout the summer, then turning

Acer palmatum
'Carlis Corner'.
Photo by Peter
Gregory.

Acer palmatum
'Chantilly Lace'.
Photo by Harold
Greer.

scarlet in the fall. 'Carlis Corner' forms a dense round shrub up to 5 ft. (1.5 m) tall and is ideal for container culture.

'Chantilly Lace'

Dissectum Group—green. This attractive laceleaf comes from Pennsylvania. The medium-sized, finely cut leaves emerge orange-red and change to a pleasant medium green for the summer, then turn golden-yellow in the fall. A second flush of leaves in midsummer is coppery red, gradually turning green. 'Chantilly Lace' is hardy and fairly vigorous, forming a mushroom-shaped mound up to 8 ft. (2.5 m) tall.

'Chirimen nishiki'

Palmatum Group—variegated. The leaves have predominant irregular yellow markings on a deep green background, often covering an entire lobe. Other markings are indistinct little areas of a subdued whitish green, with occasional flecks of light yellow. Many leaves are entirely green. The small five-lobed leaves are separated almost to the leaf base. Each lobe is very elongated, linear-lanceolate, and has an acuminate tip. The margins are irregular, wavy, and toothed. A choice but delicate plant, 'Chirimen nishiki' is not strong growing. It forms a small shrubby plant 8–10 ft. (2.5–3 m) tall at maturity. The name means "colorful crepe paper."

'Chishio'

Palmatum Group—green. The brilliant crimson spring foliage turns a medium green in the summer and in the fall develops orange-red tones of varying intensity. The moderately deeply divided leaves have five to seven narrow, ovate-lanceolate lobes with slightly toothed margins. 'Chishio' is slow growing and does not exceed 13 ft. (4 m) tall and wide. The intense orange-red new growth makes this plant as colorful as a flowering shrub. It is among the hardier cultivars and is a desirable garden plant where a small tree is needed. The name means "blood." Synonym, 'Shishio'.

'Chitose yama'

Matsumurae Group—red. The large leaves of this deeply divided red form have long narrow lobes separating almost to the leaf base. Margins are sharply toothed. New leaves are pale crimson becoming a rich purple-red in the summer, then suffused with a bronzed green before turning bright crimson in the fall. This cascading maple makes a moundlike tall shrub 10 ft. (3 m) tall and wide. It is an excellent cultivar often used in containers and occasionally for bonsai. The name means "thousand-year maple."

'Coonara Pygmy'

Dwarf Group—green. Dense and round, up to 5 ft. (1.5 m) tall and broad, this beautiful little bush has bright green leaves. The small leaves are five-lobed, each lobe broad-ovate and acuminate, with a sharp tip. The margins are toothed, sometimes bluntly so. The leaves turn a beautiful pastel yellow-orange-pink before changing to a bright deep pink in the fall, perfectly matching

Acer palmatum 'Chirimen nishiki'. Photo by J. D. Vertrees.

Acer palmatum 'Chishio'. Photo by J. D. Vertrees.

Acer palmatum 'Chitose yama'. Photo by J. D. Vertrees.

the deep coral-pink shoots. 'Coonara Pygmy' forms a natural globe shape without much pruning, is vigorous without being unruly, and has attractive foliage in all seasons. It is also valuable as a bonsai plant.

Acer palmatum 'Coonara Pygmy'. Photo by Daniel Otis.

'Corallinum'

Palmatum Group—green. The deep shrimp-pink spring foliage is very distinct and striking. In the summer, it turns green, some leaves with minute flecks or speckles of light tones. New growth later in the summer is scarlet. The small leaves are moderately deeply divided into five to seven ovate, tapered, and very slightly toothed lobes. The slender leafstalks are reddish pink. Slow growing, this cultivar makes a dense compact plant not exceeding 10 ft. (3 m) high.

'Crimson Queen'

Dissectum Group—red. The outstanding feature of this very popular cultivar is persistent good, deep red foliage color throughout the summer. Fall color is a very bright scarlet. The finely dissected leaves have narrow lobes, each deeply divided. The leafstalks are scarlet. Strong-growing, 'Crimson Queen' ages into a beautiful cascading form and reaches 10 ft. (3 m) high and 13 ft. (4 m) wide.

Acer palmatum 'Corallinum'. Photo by Peter Gregory.

Acer palmatum 'Crimson Queen'. Photo by Harold Greer.

'Demi Sec'

Dissectum Group—green. This slow-growing Dutch cultivar has deeply cut leaves similar to those of 'Green Globe', but with slight orange-tinted margins on the bright green leaves. Fall color is yellow to gold. 'Demi Sec' has an upright ball-shaped habit like that of 'Green Globe' rather than mushroom-shaped like that of most dissectums. It eventually forms a medium-sized shrub.

Acer palmatum 'Demi Sec'. Photo by Cor van Gelderen.

'Deshōjō'

Palmatum Group—red. The brilliant carmine-red spring foliage turns a light green often with reddish-bronze edges and tips for the summer. The medium-sized moderately deeply cut leaves usually have five strongly tapering lobes radiating from the center. The margins are finely toothed. This upright form makes a tall shrub of 10 ft. (3 m) and is as wide as it is tall. It is an outstanding ornamental companion plant for smaller gardens, quite desirable in the group of brilliant spring color cultivars, and often used in bonsai culture. The name can be interpreted as "the appearance of a bright red face," referring to the spring leaves.

Acer palmatum 'Deshōjō'. Photo by J. D. Vertrees.

'Dissectum Nigrum'

Dissectum Group—red. Spring growth is the distinguishing characteristic of this cultivar: the new shoots and foliage are covered with fine silvery hairs making them almost silvery gray. It soon

Acer palmatum 'Dissectum Nigrum'. Photo by J. D. Vertrees.

Acer palmatum 'Elegans'. Photo by J. D. Vertrees.

loses the pubescence and becomes a rich, deep red color. Each large leaf has seven finely dissected lobes, each lobe deeply dissected. The lobes tend to hang, giving the plant a feathery, cascading appearance. This maple holds the deep red color much longer than most red dissectums, though not quite as long as 'Crimson Queen', becoming bronze green in late summer, then turning a rich, bright red in the fall. 'Dissectum Nigrum' is vigorous growing, reaching 13–16 ft. (4–5 m) high and at least as wide. The name means "finely cut dark leaf." It can also be found under the name 'Ever Red'.

'Eddisbury'

Palmatum Group—green. A reliable and desirable coral-bark maple with leaves similar to those of the popular 'Sango kaku', 'Eddisbury' does not grow as tall and its deeper bright red shoots and leafstalks contrast with the green leaves throughout the growing season. The medium-sized leaves are mainly seven-lobed, the lobes ovate-acuminate, fine-tipped with evenly toothed margins. The slender leafstalks are bright red. New young leaves are a lighter yellow-green with red-tinged tips and edges, becoming a more uniform green in the summer. The fall colors are yellow to gold with light red overtones. This sturdy, upright plant grows vigorously when young but rarely exceeds 13 ft. (4 m) tall. Its outstanding feature is the coral-red winter shoots, the color persisting into the second and third years. The name honors the district in northwestern England where this cultivar was selected.

'Elegans'

Matsumurae Group—green. The glory of this cultivar is the fall color, a bright orange tinged with red. The medium-sized leaves have five to seven very deeply divided, widely separated, long-ovate lobes with distinctly toothed margins. The leafstalks are strong and short. This stocky-growing, low tree tends to become as wide as it is tall, 10 ft. (3 m) or more. It is a good, hardy, trouble-free plant and useful when a short tree is desired for background planting.

Acer palmatum 'Eddisbury'. Photo by Peter Gregory.

Acer palmatum 'Ellen'. Photo by Cor van Gelderen.

Acer palmatum 'Emerald Lace'. Photo by Harry Olsen.

'Ellen'

Dissectum Group—green. A vigorous, fresh green laceleaf with a very low wide-spreading growth habit, 'Ellen' reaches about 3 ft. (1 m) tall in 10 years, with a spread of 8 ft. (2.5 m). The new leaves are yellow-green, becoming medium green in the summer, then turning clear yellow in the fall. The large seven- to nine-lobed deeply dissected leaves are very variable in size. Each lobe is itself coarsely and deeply toothed. The stiff leafstalks are swollen and hooked at the base. The name honors a daughter-in-law of Dutch nurseryman D. M. van Gelderen, who selected this cultivar.

'Emerald Lace'

Dissectum Group—green. This interesting cultivar is a much deeper green than most green dissectums, has lacy foliage, and is a fast grower. The five- to seven-lobed leaves are yellow-green in the spring, darkening by midsummer, and then turning a bright burgundy red in the fall. The green leafstalks are slender but stiff. 'Emerald Lace' is vigorous growing and forms an irregular semiupright but spreading bush with long, pendulous branches. It reaches a height and spread of 10–13 ft. (3–4 m).

'Englishtown'

Dwarf Group—red. This unusual small-leaved purple-red dwarf from New Jersey arose from a witches' broom and looks somewhat like 'Shaina', but differs in its very slow, narrowly upright growth. Under normal garden conditions, it takes approximately 10 years to reach 2 ft. (60 cm) tall. The name honors the city where it was selected.

'Enkan'

Linearilobum Group—red. 'Enkan' is a small strap-leaved maple similar to 'Red Pygmy', but holding its deep wine-red coloring even better in all conditions, including the hottest climates. It is the darkest red of the linearilobums. The medium-sized five-lobed leaves are very deeply divided with the smaller basal lobes almost at right angles to the leafstalks. The straplike lobes have bluntly pointed or rounded tips and are untoothed or barely toothed. The leafstalks are purple-red.

Acer palmatum 'Englishtown'. Photo by Peter Gregory.

Acer palmatum 'Enkan'. Photo by Peter Gregory.

Acer palmatum 'Ever Autumn'. Photo by Francis Schroeder.

Acer palmatum 'Fairy Hair'. Photo by Talon Buchholz.

'Enkan' forms an upright tree of up to 10 ft. (3 m) tall. The name may be interpreted as "the tube," referring to the appearance of the leaves.

'Ever Autumn'

Palmatum Group—green. The outstanding feature of this strong upright cultivar is the flush of gold through orange-red in the otherwise rich green leaves, which lasts throughout the growing season and gives the plant its name. It culminates in quite exceptional fall coloring. The almost rounded seven- to nine-lobed leaves are fairly deeply divided with the lower lobes pointing sideways. Each lobe is broadly ovate with a short tail-like pointed tip and coarsely toothed margins.

'Fairy Hair'

Dwarf Group—green. An intriguing dwarf laceleaf that reaches 3 ft. (1 m) tall, 'Fairy Hair', as the name implies, develops very thin, threadlike leaves that tend to be bunched together. It does not develop the broader palmate leaves characteristic of the more vigorous 'Koto-no-ito'. The spring leaves are an attractive orange-red, becoming green for the summer.

'Fall's Fire'

Matsumurae Group—green. This aptly named cultivar is noted for its spectacular display of yellows, oranges, reds, and purples in the fall. The medium-sized seven-lobed palmate leaves are an attractive yellow-green in the spring. The plant is vigorous and soon forms an upright medium-sized tree.

'Fascination'

Matsumurae Group—green. This vigorous growing, upright, rounded tree has large, very deeply divided leaves which are edged with large narrow teeth. The leaves are similar to those of 'Omure yama'. They emerge yellow-orange in the spring, becoming medium green for summer, and turning orange-red in the fall. This cultivar has attractive green bark with white striations, giving it a conspicuous gray-green appearance.

Acer palmatum 'Fall's Fire'. Photo by Francis Schroeder.

Acer palmatum 'Fascination'. Photo by Harold Greer.

'Felice'

Dissectum Group—red. An outstanding red-leaved dissectum, 'Felice' has two unusual features: the leaves bunch up at intervals along the shoots, causing the yellowish young leaves to look like brush tips, and the seven-lobed deeply dissected red leaves are of two kinds. One type of leaf has lobes that narrow near the leaf base to little more than the width of the midrib, with the lobes themselves deeply incised. The other type of leaf has broader, much less deeply divided lobules, sometimes little more than large teeth. The margins have coarse, sharply pointed teeth. The

Acer palmatum
'Felice'. Photo by
Cor van Gelderen.

Acer palmatum
'Filigree'. Photo by
J. D. Vertrees.

red leafstalks are short and sturdy. The new leaves emerge a light yellow-green with pink edging, becoming a bronze-green with reddish-purple edging. The bunches of young yellow leaves against the darker purple-green older foliage give a pleasant multicolored effect. 'Felice' forms a bushy mound estimated to reach a height and spread of about 10 ft. (3 m).

'Filigree'

Dissectum Group—variegated. The feathery look and interesting color changes make this small maple a conversation piece. The base color of the leaves is light green, almost yellow-green in the spring, darkening as the season progresses. Overlaid on this is a profusion of minute dots, specks, or flecks of pale gold or cream. Fall color is a rich gold. The bark of the shoots and branches is silvery green with definite white striping or flecking. The large seven-lobed, sharply pointed leaves are dissected entirely to the base, each lobe delicately and deeply dissected making a very lacy leaf. 'Filigree' is compact and makes a well-rounded, cascading plant 6½ ft. (2 m) high and 10 ft. (3 m) wide. It is a very desirable cultivar for landscapers and collectors.

'Fior d'Arancio'

Matsumurae Group—red. The leaves are similar in shape and size to those of 'Wakehurst Pink', without the variegation and with chunkier, less-hooked teeth on the margins. The foliage emerges a bright orange-red, becoming bronze and copper red. It tends to green up easily when shaded. The contrast of orange-red young leaves on a background of copper-green older leaves produces an attractive multicolor effect. The large seven-lobed leaves are deeply divided. Each ovate lobe has a long, pointed tip and conspicuously toothed margins. The stiff leafstalks are reddish bronze. This cultivar forms an upright rounded tree up to 20 ft. (6 m) high. It is named by an Italian nursery for a variety of grape from the same area which produces an orange-colored wine.

'First Ghost'

Matsumurae Group—variegated. This sport of 'Beni shigitatsu sawa' has similarly large deeply divided leaves, with irregular wavy margins and coarse, sharp teeth. It differs in the pale white leaf base color with a contrasting dark green network of veins. The leaf edges may be lightly pink tinged when first appearing. Fall colors are orange to gold. The ghostlike leaves are supported by the gray-white young shoots. This interesting cultivar forms a small to medium-sized tree estimated to grow up to 13 ft. (4 m) tall. It needs some protection from the afternoon sun.

Acer palmatum 'Fior d'Arancio'. Photo by Cor van Gelderen.

Acer palmatum 'First Ghost'. Photo by Talon Buchholz.

Acer palmatum 'Flavescens'. Photo by J. D. Vertrees.

Acer palmatum 'Garyū'. Photo by Peter Gregory.

Acer palmatum 'Garnet'. Photo by J. D. Vertrees.

'Garnet'

Dissectum Group—red. The outstanding features are leaf color and plant vigor. The leaf color, which is the rich red-orange of the gemstone garnet, develops well in sunny situations. The leaves are large for a dissectum, with the seven lobes separate entirely to the base, each lobe not as deeply cut as in most dissectums, and the leaf appears coarser. The plant is vigorous-growing and eventually attains a height of 13 ft. (4 m) or more. As it matures it forms a beautiful, cascading, mound-shaped specimen. It retains color well and is a durable landscape plant.

'Flavescens'

Dissectum Group—green. The distinct yellow-green foliage makes this cultivar worthwhile. The green tones of the large leaves darken as summer progresses. Fall color is yellow, occasionally tinged orange. The five to seven deeply separated lobes are incised and toothed along the margins but not as deeply cut to the midrib as in most dissectums. This plant is very vigorous and matures at 8 ft. (2.5 m) high and 10 ft. (3 m) wide. The name means "yellowish."

'Garyū'

Dwarf Group—green. The small medium green to light green leaves have three to five very narrow lobes separated almost entirely to the base. The lobes are elongate-lanceolate, tapering to a narrow tip. They twist sideways, curl up or down, or become slightly sickle-shaped. The margins are complex—deeply toothed to lobulate or combinations of both. The entire appearance of the foliage is disorganized but attractive. New leaves have a red overtone, which may persist around the margins. This compact dwarf is semiprostrate in habit. It eventually reaches about 3 ft. (1 m) high and wide. The name means "one's own style or manner," aptly describing this cultivar's distinctive foliage.

'Geisha'

Palmatum Group—variegated. In the spring, the deeply divided leaves are delicate shades of pink to light cream, sparsely flecked with dark green and medium green spots and small patches. The creamy areas turn a pale yellow-green and the main veins become green in the summer, but the attractive pink tones persist. The medium-sized leaves are divided into five to seven narrowly ovate lobes with tail-like pointed tips and coarsely toothed margins. The leaves are intermediate in shape between palmate and straplike. The short, slender leafstalks are pink. 'Geisha' is a slow-growing bushy tree, eventually reaching 8 ft. (2.5 m) tall. It is distinct, unusual, and somewhat delicate, needing protection and semishade. It makes a fine patio plant and is ideal for containers. The name means "young dancing girl."

'Germaine's Gyration'

Dissectum Group—green. This laceleaf grows more vigorously than most dissectums, so the long cascading branches twist and are wavy, giving rise to the "gyration" half of the name. The large, coarse seven- to nine-lobed, dissected leaves are again cut into sublobes but not as deeply as in most dissectums. The sublobes themselves are coarsely toothed. The dark green summer foliage changes to a beautiful yellow, orange, and red in the fall. This plant forms a cascading mushroom-shaped mound, much wider than tall. The name honors Germaine Iseli of the famed Oregon nursery family.

'Golden Pond'

Amoenum Group—green. This cultivar has the same stunning deep yellow-orange fall color as 'Hōgyoku', with the leaves similar in shape but smaller. The summer color is a medium green.

Acer palmatum 'Geisha'. Photo by Peter Gregory.

Acer palmatum 'Germaine's Gyration'. Photo by Harry Olsen.

Acer palmatum 'Golden Pond'. Photo by Peter Gregory.

Acer palmatum 'Goshiki kotohime'. Photo by J. D. Vertrees.

Acer palmatum 'Goshiki shidare'. Photo by Peter Gregory.

The growth habit is exactly opposite that of 'Hōgyoku', about one and a half times as wide as tall—14½ ft. (4.5 m) wide and 10 ft. (3 m) tall.

'Goshiki kotohime'

Dwarf Group—variegated. A beautiful variegated form of the excellent dwarf 'Kotohime', 'Goshiki kotohime' produces very small irregularly shaped leaves which are deeply divided and have very coarsely toothed margins. New leaves are pink-red with green veins, with the variegation in tiny flecks and speckles of varying inten-

sity. The developing leaves become green with white to creamy variegation, forming a contrasting background to the pink-red new leaves which are produced all summer. This cultivar forms a slow-growing dense compact small bush less than 3 ft. (1 m) tall. It is ideal for the rock garden and containers. The name means "dwarf multicolored old harp."

'Goshiki shidare'

Dissectum Group—variegated. Like 'Toyama nishiki', this cascading laceleaf has variegated leaves. Some are in various shades of green with dark red overtones. Other leaves have thin lobes twisted, curled, and almost tangled. These are deep red-green, heavily marked with pink or white. All degrees of variations of the above may be present. The leaf is smaller than that of most dissectums. The name means "cascading multicolors" and refers to the color of the leaves.

'Green Globe'

Dissectum Group—green. Unlike most dissectums which have a pendulous habit, this dissectum forms a rounded ball shape. The spring color is an attractive rose, turning to shades of creamy white, quickly becoming a fresh emerald green for the summer before turning bright yellow in the fall. The shoots and leafstalks are an attractive medium green. The seven-lobed leaves are deeply dissected to the base. The lobes themselves are fairly deeply divided. This vigorous-growing cultivar is estimated to reach a height of 13–16 ft. (4–5 m) at maturity, with a spread of 10–13 ft. (3–4 m).

'Green Hornet'

Dissectum Group—green. With finely cut lacy leaves, 'Green Hornet' has the distinction of being the only green dissectum with outstanding red fall color. The spring leaves are green, tinged orange, changing to a fresh green for the summer, before turning a beautiful bright red in the fall. The green summer foliage contrasts attractively with the green flushed-orange new growth appearing throughout the summer.

Acer palmatum 'Green Globe'. Photo by Cor van Gelderen.

Acer palmatum 'Green Hornet'. Photo by Francis Schroeder.

Acer palmatum 'Green Lace'.
Photo by Cor van Gelderen.

Acer palmatum 'Green Mist'.
Photo by Cor van Gelderen.

Acer palmatum 'Green Star'.
Photo by Peter Gregory.

'Green Hornet' is very vigorous early on with long sweeping pendulous shoots, and forms a wide-spreading mushroom-shaped mound up to 10 ft. (3 m) tall.

'Green Lace'

Dissectum Group—green. Desirable for its fine leaf texture, graceful pendulous shape, and outstanding fall color, 'Green Lace' grows into a wide mushroom-shaped mound, 10–13 ft. (3–4 m) tall and broad, and can be planted in full sun or partial shade. The deeply dissected leaves have lobes themselves divided to the midrib. These sublobes are strongly toothed. The new leaves emerge a light creamy green, becoming a light emerald green for the summer. In the fall, their color is a beautiful clear golden-yellow.

'Green Mist'

Dissectum Group—green. This excellent medium green laceleaf is similar to 'Waterfall' in leaf and habit but with orange-red fall color and greater hardiness. The large seven-lobed leaves are deeply divided almost to the midrib and have margins with narrow, sharply pointed, curved teeth. 'Green Mist' is vigorous and forms a cascading mound up to 10 ft. (3 m) high. The color and delicate appearance of the pendulous foliage give the plant a soft misty look for which it is named.

'Green Star'

Amoenum Group—green. The leaf and habit of this large vigorous upright cultivar are similar to the ever-popular 'Ōsakazuki', but the leaves, instead of turning scarlet, become a brilliant orange in the fall. They are medium-sized with five broad, moderately deeply divided green lobes and finely and evenly toothed margins. New growth is yellow-green with an attractive light blush of pink-red, especially on the margins.

'Green Trompenburg'

Matsumurae Group—green. The distinctive green leaves of this tall-growing cultivar are almost identical in shape to those of the well-known red-leaved 'Trompenburg'. The color is a dark, rich green and does not appear to sunburn.

Acer palmatum 'Green Trompenburg'. Photo by Cor van Gelderen.

Acer palmatum 'Groundcover'. Photo by Francis Schroeder.

Acer palmatum 'Hagoromo'. Photo by J. D. Vertrees.

The new leaves carry a shading of rusty red on the tips and edges, which soon disappears. Fall colors are orange and yellow. The medium-sized leaves have seven to nine lobes radiating outward in almost a complete circle and are deeply separated. Each lobe is long and slender, with rolled-down edges, making a long semitube. Strong leafstalks hold the leaf outward. This interesting, very vigorous tree reaches about 26 ft. (8 m) tall. As with 'Trompenburg', the leaf shape is unusual and attractive. This green form gives an added choice for the landscape. Named for an arboretum in Rotterdam, Netherlands.

'Groundcover'

Dwarf Group—green. The small leaves of this useful dwarf have five narrow deeply divided lobes. The lobes are narrow-ovate with long, pointed tips and large coarsely toothed margins. The leafstalks are short and threadlike. The foliage is medium green with the leaf tips and outer margins tinged pink to red-bronze. This cultivar is aptly named, growing into a very dense twiggy plant which hugs the ground. It reaches 2 ft. (60 cm) tall and 3–3½ ft. (1–1.2 m) wide.

'Hagoromo'

Other Group—green. The very unusual and distinctive medium-sized leaf has five lobes completely divided to the base and attached directly to the shoot without a leafstalk. The lobes are broadly lanceolate with their bases quickly tapering to stalklike attachments. The margins are coarsely toothed. Each leaf and lobe has a different plane of attitude, twisting and curving to give a very feathery appearance. Leaf color is dark green, with emerging young leaves tinged pink. Fall colors are a blend of light yellows and oranges. This cultivar has a narrow, dense upright form, slowly reaching about 20 ft. (6 m) high. The name means "Japanese angel's dress."

'Hazeroino' resembles 'Hagoromo' with similar stalkless but variegated leaves. It is not as strong growing, however, eventually reaching a height of 10 ft. (3 m) or so.

Acer palmatum 'Hanami nishiki'.
Photo by J. D. Vertrees.

Acer palmatum 'Harusame'.
Photo by J. D. Vertrees.

'Momenshide' leaves look very much like those of 'Hagoromo'—small with practically no leafstalks (only a few millimeters long) and attached almost directly to the twig—but 'Momenshide' is a taller plant.

'Hanami nishiki'

Dwarf Group—green. The light yellow-green leaves have lightly bronzed edges and tips in the spring. They are moderately deeply divided into three to five lobes which radiate outward. Each lobe sharply tapers to a point and has lightly toothed margins. The short leafstalks are very thin and delicate. The spring leaves are orange-red, particularly along the margins, becoming a uniform light to yellowish green. In the garden, the plant can eventually reach 6½ ft. (2 m) tall

and wide, but is much smaller if container grown. This maple, though slightly delicate, is one of the real gems of the dwarf group. It is among the smallest-leaved forms. The name means "flower-viewing tapestry."

'Harusame'

Palmatum Group—green. 'Harusame' is best known for its fall color, when the red is dusted with yellowish-brown indistinct markings. For most of the year, the small five- to seven-lobed leaves are a light green. The lanceolate-ovate lobes are moderately deeply divided and coarsely toothed. This plant makes an upright, bushy, small tree. It does not reach much more than 10 ft. (3 m) tall and wide. The name means "spring rain."

Acer palmatum 'Herbstfeuer'. Photo by Cor van Gelderen.

'Herbstfeuer'

Matsumurae Group—green. Probably a cross between *Acer palmatum* and *A. circinatum*, this cultivar has seven- to nine-lobed circular leaves with broadly ovate lobes and pointed tips. The stiff stout leafstalks are red. The leaves are dark green during the summer, becoming green with bronze and purple tones in late summer. In the fall, this German cultivar comes into its own, turning an outstanding orange. It is very vigorous, densely branched, upright, wide-spreading, and reaching 16–20 ft. (5–6 m) tall and about as wide. The name means "autumn fire."

Acer palmatum 'Hessei'. Photo by Peter Gregory.

'Hessei'

Matsumurae Group—red. The seven-lobed, very deeply divided leaves are medium-sized. Each lobe is long and narrow with toothed margins. The leaves droop slightly and give the plant a ribbonlike effect. Leaf color from spring to early summer is a rich purple-red, changing later to greenish bronze. Fall color is a brilliant crimson. 'Hessei' is hardy and strong but not tall-standing, tending to spread, and reaching about 16 ft. (5 m) high and 13 ft. (4 m) wide.

'Higasa yama'
Popcorn maple

Matsumurae—variegated. A long-established favorite, 'Higasa yama' is quite stunning in the spring when the buds unfold to reveal pale cream tightly curled leaflets surrounded by brilliant crimson elongated bud scales. The effect is of two-toned popcorn. Leaf color is very changeable. The developing leaves have light green central veins bordered in dark green and surrounded by cream-colored margins with pink tones at first, becoming creamy-green. In the fall, the cream portions take on an orange to dark yellow and occasionally red tone. The unusually shaped moderately deeply divided leaves have seven slender, elongate lobes which taper to a sharp point. The margins are strongly toothed. Usually the leaves are crinkly and curl upward, but some are slightly twisted or curl downward. When suppressed in pots, 'Higasa yama' is quite dense and

Acer palmatum 'Higasa yama'. Photo by J. D. Vertrees.

lends itself to shaping, making it popular for bonsai. It is hardy in the garden landscape, where it has a narrow upright habit reaching 23–26 ft. (7–8 m) tall. The unique growth habit and foliage make it very attractive. The name means "the umbrella mountain."

'Hiryū'

Palmatum Group—variegated. The main characteristic of this Japanese cultivar is the very unusual distorted foliage. The size and shape of the leaves depend on the amount of variegation. The small leaves have five narrow deeply divided lobes with crinkly edges. All the lobes point forward. Leaves with very little or no variegation are larger with much broader lobes. In the spring, the leaves are green with red-brown tips, becoming mid to dark green with varying widths of gray-green to light green edging for the summer. Fall color is orange to red. This strange-leaved cultivar forms an upright vase-shaped tree up to 13 ft. (4 m) tall. The name means "flying dragon."

Acer palmatum 'Hiryū'. Photo by Cor van Gelderen.

'Hōgyoku'

Amoenum Group—green. 'Hōgyoku' was selected for its rich, deep orange fall color. The spring and summer foliage is a deep, rich green. The large leaves have seven lobes which radiate out and are divided only up to halfway to the base. They are ovate-triangular with finely toothed margins. This sturdy and hardy cultivar reaches 16–20 ft. (5–6 m) tall. It is a worthwhile plant, since most of the year it is an attractive rich green, followed by the unique orange of fall. The name means "a jewel."

Acer palmatum 'Hōgyoku'. Photo by Daniel Otis.

'Hoshi kuzu'

Dwarf Group—variegated. The small unusual five-lobed leaves are star-shaped. Each lobe varies in shape according to the degree of variegation and is mostly long and slender, slightly broader in the middle, and gradually tapering to a fine tip which tends to turn down. The margins are faintly toothed. Leaf color is a pleasant light green. In each leaf, there are variegated breaks of varying size and shape. Some leaves are totally pale cream green, others may only have one lobe variegated on the edge. The cream-green may be faintly pink-tinged in the spring. This neat-growing, upright, non-spreading, small shrub blends well with many types of companions and makes a good patio plant. The name means "star-studded sky."

'Hupp's Dwarf'

Dwarf Group—green. A choice green dwarf similar to 'Kotohime', 'Mikawa yatsubusa', and 'Tsukomo', 'Hupp's Dwarf' is more compact than these and more vigorous than 'Tsukomo'. The fo-

Acer palmatum 'Hoshi kuzu'. Photo by Cor van Gelderen.

Acer palmatum 'Hupp's Dwarf'. Photo by Cor van Gelderen.

liage is a deep, rich green. The leaf has five long, slender, deeply divided lobes with sharp, slender points and with strongly toothed margins. The leaves are densely concentrated on the short annual growth. Because of its minimal annual growth, this cultivar is ideal for bonsai.

'Ibo nishiki'

Palmatum Group—green. This tall-growing plant is one of the rough-barked cultivars. The wartiness develops slowly, appearing on third-year (or older) wood, and joining into larger roughened areas after a few years. The intermediate bark color is a good green. The medium-sized leaves are five- to seven-lobed and fairly deeply separated. The lobes are long-ovate with heavily toothed margins. Spring color is a good light green with bronze-tinged margins. Fall colors range from yellow-orange to deep crimson. This

Acer palmatum 'Ibo nishiki'. Photo by J. D. Vertrees.

fairly strong grower has the upright habit characteristic of the Palmatum Group. The warty bark is an interest point for the collector of unusual forms. The name means "warty rough bark."

Acer palmatum 'Ichigyōji'. Photo by J. D. Vertrees.

'Ichigyōji'

Amoenum Group—green. Except for its intense brilliant yellow or orange fall color, 'Ichigyōji' resembles the crimson-leaved 'Ōsakazuki'. During summer, the large seven-lobed leaves are a pleasant green. They are broadly ovate and sharp-pointed, with slightly toothed edges. The lobes are joined about halfway to the base. The tree is upright and broad and becomes round-headed, reaching a height of 23 ft. (7 m). Japanese writers advise planting 'Ichigyōji' and 'Ōsakazuki' near each other to allow the full glory of the fall brilliance to be appreciated. 'Ichigyōji' is named after a temple.

'Iijima sunago'

Matsumurae Group—variegated. The colors of this dark-leaved cultivar make it an unusual addition to the garden landscape. The large leaves have seven deeply divided, broadly ovate lobes with clearly toothed margins. Spring foliage is a rich red, slightly on the orange side, becoming a rich purplish brown—a rather unique color—with tiny, irregular green spots, resembling sprinkled sand. It is this type of variegation, known as *sunago fu* (sand-dusted), that gives this cultivar its name. The midribs remain a distinctly contrasting yellow-green, while the leaves turn to yellows, oranges, and reds in the fall. This strong-growing round-headed tree remains upright and matures at about 23–26 ft. (7–8 m) high. The name means "dusted Iijima," referring to the leaf variegation and the site of a shrine associated with the cultivar.

Acer palmatum 'Iijima sunago'. Photo by J. D. Vertrees.

'Inazuma'

Matsumurae Group—red. The large leaves are of a rich, deep purple-red with green veins in the spring and early summer. As they mature, they become a dark purple with green tinges, eventually turning a stunning bright red-crimson in the fall. The deeply divided leaves have seven long, ovate-lanceolate, widely separated lobes

Acer palmatum 'Inazuma'. Photo by J. D. Vertrees.

with clearly toothed margins. This hardy cultivar is vigorous and forms a tall, rounded shrub or tree with cascading foliage, up to 33 ft. (10 m) high and 16–20 ft. (5–6 m) wide. The name means "thunderer."

'Irish Lace'

Dissectum Group—green. The outstanding feature of this cultivar is the bright orange-pink young foliage, which becomes green with pink then bronzed edges and tips, and turning orange-red in the fall. This coloration, added to the pleated and rumpled leaf lobes, gives the plant a charm of its own. The orange-pink new growth overlying the older green leaves continues throughout the summer. The medium-sized seven-lobed leaves are deeply dissected. The lobes are also deeply dissected and have slender, hooked, sharply pointed teeth along the margins. The reddish leafstalks are long and slender. 'Irish Lace' grows into the typical dissectum cascading mound up to about 8 ft. (2.5 m) tall at maturity.

'Issai nishiki'

Dwarf Group—green. 'Issai nishiki' is similar to 'Nishiki gawa' but smaller and with extremely rough bark. Unlike 'Nishiki gawa', it develops the bark characteristics within a year of propagation, becoming rougher with each season. The name means "develops rough bark within a year."

Acer palmatum 'Irish Lace'. Photo by Harold Greer.

Acer palmatum 'Issai nishiki'. Photo by Peter Gregory.

Acer palmatum 'Japanese Sunrise'. Photo by Harold Greer.

Acer palmatum 'Jirō shidare'. Photo by Peter Gregory.

Acer palmatum 'Johin'. Photo by Talon Buchholz.

'Japanese Sunrise'

Palmatum Group—green. 'Japanese Sunrise' is similar to 'Sango kaku' but with lighter red winter shoots on the upper exposed side and yellow-orange on the lower sheltered side. The leaves emerge yellow-green, becoming a light fresh green for the summer. The fall colors are yellow, gold, and crimson tones. 'Japanese Sunrise' is very tolerant of full sun and grows into an upright, wide, flat-topped tree, up to 23 ft. (7 m) tall.

'Jirō shidare'

Palmatum Group—green. This cascading form has smallish bright green leaves with mainly seven moderately deeply divided ovate-elliptic lobes. The margins are clearly toothed. The brilliant crimson fall coloration is striking. With age, the long slender branches tend to droop, down to the ground in some cases, resulting in a round-headed bush up to 10 ft. (3 m) tall and wide. The

leaf nodes, which are spread far apart on the slender, pendulous shoots, form the cascading growth and give a very lacy appearance. This maple is a nice addition to the larger rock garden. The name means "white cascading."

'Johin'

Matsumurae Group—red. The beautiful burnished coppery-red leaves have contrasting yellow-green main veins that persist for most of the season. The nine-lobed leaves are very similar to those of the well-known 'Trompenburg', with toothed slightly rolled margins, but not as deeply divided. This very attractive medium-sized tree comes from Oregon. The name means "elegant."

'Johnnie's Pink'

Palmatum Group—red. The unusual but attractive semiglossy, bronze-red, hawthornlike leaves make this cultivar most desirable. The small leaves

Acer palmatum
'Johnnie's Pink'. Photo by
Harry Olsen.

Acer palmatum
'Kaba'. Photo by
Cor van Gelderen.

have five broad lobes divided about halfway to the base. The margins are relatively large-toothed. The center lobe is often dominant. The leaves become bronze-green later in the summer. This cultivar forms a small round shrub and is ideal for small gardens, patios and containers.

'Kaba'

Dwarf Group—green. This strange-leafed small compact upright dwarf grows to about 2 ft. (60 cm) in five years or so. It resembles a dwarf form of 'Wabito' with similar dark green leaves. These

are small and very deeply divided into fine narrow almost straplike lobes. The often red-tinged margins are unevenly and bluntly toothed and crinkled. The name means "hippopotamus," a play on the name of the English nursery from where it originated.

'Kagerō'

Amoenum Group—variegated. The distinguishing feature of this outstanding cultivar is the predominantly yellow variegation instead of white as in most variegates. The leaves are deeply di-

Acer palmatum 'Kagerō'.
Photo by J. D. Vertrees.

Acer palmatum 'Kagiri
nishiki'. Photo by J. D.
Vertrees.

vided into five to seven radiating lobes. Each lobe is elongate-ovate with a long, tapering tip and finely toothed margins. The variegations are irregular, blending in various patterns on a rich green base. The light markings may consist of only a few irregular specks on a leaf, small light blotches, or solid areas. Sometimes the colors occupy only half the lobe or entirely green leaves occur, and occasionally solid yellow leaves. This fairly strong, hardy but slow-growing, upright cultivar forms a short tree up to 13 ft. (4 m) tall. The name means "gossamer."

'Kagiri nishiki'

Palmatum Group—variegated. Each small leaf is different and each of the five to seven lobes per leaf is a different shape. The typical lobe is elongate-ovate, tapering to a sharp point. Edges are slightly and inconsistently toothed, some lightly notched. The lobes are sickle-shaped to varying degrees, depending upon the amount of variegation. The leafstalks are slender and pink. Leaf color is deep green with a bluish cast, never bright green. Light cream margins on all the lobes are present in varying widths. The variegations

Acer palmatum 'Kamagata'. Photo by J. D. Vertrees.

are suffused with pink or rose in the spring, becoming cream in the summer, and turning a vivid rose-crimson in the fall. The plant is somewhat open growing but upright and can reach 26 ft. (8 m) tall. It differs from 'Butterfly' in having more rose in the leaf markings, and its leaf margins are not toothed as deeply.

'Kamagata'

Dwarf Group—green. Delicate looking, this very durable dwarf is hardy, even in exposed positions with full sun, and on very dry sites. The small, deeply divided leaves are mainly five-lobed. The lobes are sickle-shaped or downward-curved at the tip and curve gently upward at the sides to form a shallow trough. Each lobe is long and narrow, tapering gradually to a sharp point. The margins are toothed. Leafstalks are very thin but stiff, and young shoots are a bright green. In the spring, leaf edges are strongly tinted with red to rusty red, becoming a bright, light green in the summer. Fall colors are brilliant yellow and orange, with an occasional touch of red. The leaves remain on the plant well into late fall and thus extend the color period. 'Kamagata' forms a small, rounded bush. The name refers to the hooked tips on the leaves.

'Kandy Kitchen'

Dwarf Group—red. New leaves form a bright pink-red bunch at the end of the shoots, contrasting with the purple-red of the mature leaves throughout summer. Fall color is a very bright scarlet-red. This cultivar, from a witches' broom, forms a compact rounded shrub reaching up to 6½ ft. (2 m) tall and wide. It is ideal for containers.

'Elizabeth' is similar in growth, leaf shape, color, and size to 'Kandy Kitchen' but has a narrower, more upright habit.

'Karaori nishiki'

Palmatum Group—variegated. The medium-sized variegated leaves have five to seven moderately deeply divided oblong-ovate lobes with toothed margins. Spring foliage is reddish, changing to a greenish red in midsummer. The

Acer palmatum 'Kandy Kitchen'. Photo by Harry Olsen.

Acer palmatum 'Karaori nishiki'. Photo by Peter Gregory.

whitish variegations range from indistinct to very bold and sometimes have a pink overtone. These variegations are yellowish in midseason. Fall color is crimson. 'Karaori nishiki' forms a tall bush up to 13 ft. (4 m) high. It is not a vigorous cultivar and grows rather slowly. The name refers to a type of brocade used for dancers' garments.

Acer palmatum 'Kasagi yama'. Photo by J. D. Vertrees.

Acer palmatum 'Kasen nishiki'. Photo by J. D. Vertrees.

Acer palmatum 'Kashima'. Photo by Peter Gregory.

'Kasagi yama'

Matsumurae Group—variegated. The leaves of this unusual cultivar have a unique brick-red color varying during the season and with the growing conditions. Leaf margins and veins are tinged dark greenish red to almost black. The changing color in the spring is very exciting. Bright red fruits complement the leaf colors. The medium-sized leaves have seven very deeply divided lobes radiating evenly outwards like a star. Each lobe is long-ovate with a long, sharp tapering point and finely but sharply toothed margins. The red leafstalks are short and stiff. This cultivar forms an open-crowned shrub or small tree up to 23 ft. (7 m) tall. The name means "overhanging mountain."

'Kasen nishiki'

Palmatum Group—variegated. Spring foliage is often a surprising pink-red or light orange-red, which soon matures into variegated greens. Variegation is quite subtle and soft-toned, with irregular sections of white or cream on many leaves. These portions are usually sickle-shaped. Most leaves have a very light or pastel speckling and dotting of white, cream, or occasionally whitish green. This cultivar is quite different from most variegated cultivars. The medium-sized leaves have five to seven moderately deeply divided lobes. Each lobe is ovate-acuminate, with definite toothed edges. This small bushy tree may eventually reach 20 ft. (6 m). It is a hardy cultivar and well worth its place in the garden landscape.

'Kashima'

Dwarf Group—green. The tiny rich green leaves are moderately deeply divided into five lobes, with a prominent center lobe. Each lobe is elongate-ovate, terminating in a sharp point. The margins are toothed. The leafstalks are very slender. Spring leaves are a very light yellow-green, with margins a brick or rust color. Fall color is yellow. This plant is hardy and a very shrubby grower, usually less than 1 m tall, but it can reach up to 6½ ft. (2 m) tall and wide. It is ideal for rock gardens and takes well to shaping and pruning. This dwarf form is widely used for bonsai. It is named after a well-known Japanese shrine.

'Katsura'

Palmatum Group—green. This delightful form is quite striking in its spring growth, when leaves are a pale yellow-orange with margins shading into a brighter orange. The leaves turn a light green to yellow-green for summer. Fall colors are bright yellow and orange. The small leaves have five ovate-lanceolate lobes, tapering to a long point, and fairly deeply separated. The margins are shallowly toothed. The center lobe is always longer. This cultivar grows into a dense upright tree, up to 16 ft. (5 m) tall. It adapts well to bonsai culture. The name means "wig."

'Kihachijō'

Matsumurae Group—green. The large seven- to nine-lobed leaves are a bright green, and the lobes are long-ovate with conspicuous deeply toothed margins. The very narrow tip of each lobe gives a distinctive effect. Fall color is unique—a distinct yellow-gold blended with light orange and reds. The bark is a strong green with white streaking and an overtone of bluish gray. This

Acer palmatum 'Katsura'. Photo by Peter Gregory.

Acer palmatum 'Kihachijō'. Photo by Peter Gregory.

Acer palmatum 'Kingsville Variegated'. Photo by Cor van Gelderen.

Acer palmatum 'Kinran'. Photo by J. D. Vertrees.

Acer palmatum 'Kinshi'. Photo by Harry Olsen.

good, hardy, sturdy cultivar develops into a well-rounded, short tree or tall bush up to 20 ft. (6 m) high. It adds a "different" appearance for landscaping. The name means "from Hachijo Island."

'Kingsville Variegated'

Palmatum Group—variegated. Intermediate between 'Kagiri nishiki' and 'Butterfly', this selection has a basic leaf color of deep green or blue-green. Variegation is irregular, mostly white with a noticeable amount of pink. Occasionally, the pink markings cover almost the entire leaf. The white portions become a brilliant rose in the fall. The small five-lobed leaves are irregular, each lobe long and narrow with very irregularly toothed margins, quite different from the margins of 'Butterfly' or 'Kagiri nishiki'. The growth rate and habit are similar to 'Kagiri nishiki'. This cultivar is a delightful companion to some of the other variegated forms. It was named after the city where the nursery which selected it was located.

'Kinran'

Matsumurae Group—red. The medium-sized leaves are deeply divided into seven lobes which are separated almost to the usually flat leaf base.

Each lobe is long-ovate with a long, narrow tip and strongly toothed margins. The leaves have an open, lacy appearance. The spring and early summer coloration is a deep, rich bronze-red, with the midveins a contrasting yellow-green. In late summer, the color changes to a deep green shaded dark red. Fall color is a beautiful gold tinged with crimson. This sturdy, hardy plant only reaches 10 ft. (3 m) in 10–15 years and broadens out to form a round-topped, large bush. It makes a good container plant. The name means "woven with golden strings," referring to the fall color of the leaves.

'Kinshi'

Linearilobum Group—green. Wonderful orange-yellow fall color characterizes this semidwarf strapleaf. The five- to seven-lobed medium to dark green leaves are divided to the base and have pointed tips and sparsely shallow-toothed margins. The green leafstalks are short and slender. 'Kinshi' forms a tidy, compact, upright tree, attaining a height of 8 ft. (2.5 m). It would be at home in most gardens whatever their size and is perfectly suited for containers. The name means "with golden threads," referring to the fall leaf color.

Acer palmatum 'Kiyohime'. Photo by Peter Gregory.

Acer palmatum 'Kogane nishiki'. Photo by Harold Greer.

Acer palmatum 'Kiri nishiki'. Photo by Peter Gregory.

'Kiri nishiki'

Dissectum Group—green. The nine-lobed, coarsely dissected leaves are a bright, light green which stands full sun well. In the fall, the intense gold color is excellent, occasionally suffused with crimson and scarlet on the tips. This plant is fairly strong growing and hardy. Like many pendulous dissectums, it should be planted on a bank or grafted high to realize the full effect of the beautifully cascading display. It reaches 10 ft. (3 m) high and wide. The name means "misty brocade."

'Kiyohime'

Dwarf Group—green. Each small leaf is five-lobed, with the center lobe noticeably longer. The lobes are ovate-lanceolate and deeply divided. The sharp lobe tips tend to turn downward. The margins are toothed. The leafstalks are a rich green tinged with pink. Early spring leaves are beautiful. The edges are tinged with orange-red, which is lightly and delicately shaded into the light green leaf center. The summer foliage is a rich green, turning yellow-orange in the fall. 'Kiyohime' is a sturdy, vigorous plant, suitable for container and bonsai culture. It can form a dense roundish bush 6½ ft. (2 m) high. The name means "yellow-leaved dwarf."

'Kogane nishiki'

Palmatum Group—green. 'Kogane nishiki' is a strong-growing tree for background or overstory plantings. The medium-sized five- to seven-lobed leaves are a deep, rich green. The lobes are long-ovate with acuminate points and are fairly deeply separated. The edges are lightly toothed. Spring leaves have yellow tips, then change to a strong

Acer palmatum 'Kogane sakae'. Photo by J. D. Vertrees.

Acer palmatum 'Komachi hime'. Photo by Cor van Gelderen.

Acer palmatum 'Komon nishiki'. Photo by J. D. Vertrees.

green for summer. Fall color is a bright gold. This tree reaches 33 ft. (10 m) in 20 years. It makes a good base plant for landscapes, and the golden fall color can work as a contrast to other plantings. A site in full sun is best. The name means "golden brocade."

'Kogane sakae'

Amoenum Group—green. 'Kogane sakae' is an unusual tree notable for its bark color. The young shoots and older branches are light green with striations and irregular streaks of a yellowish tone. The leaves are medium to large, seven-lobed, and separated halfway to the base, with the ovate lobes widest at the midpoint. Margins are finely toothed. The leaves are a bright green with reddish tips in the spring. Fall colors are pale orange to yellow. This strong, upright-growing tree is of good stature, reaching 33–43 ft. (10–13 m) tall. The name means "golden prosperity."

'Komachi hime'

Dwarf Group—green. A lovely very slow growing dwarf from the United States, 'Komachi hime' is very similar in leaf and habit to the better-known 'Kiyohime'. The small five-lobed leaves are light green with bright red tips and margins in the spring, becoming medium green with darker red tips in the summer. The lobes are sharply pointed and radiate outwards to give the leaves a starlike appearance. The name means "beautiful little girl."

'Komon nishiki'

Palmatum Group—variegated. The small leaves are fairly deeply divided into five to seven ovate-acuminate lobes which gradually taper to

Acer palmatum 'Korean Gem'. Photo by J. D. Vertrees.

Acer palmatum 'Koshibori nishiki'. Photo by Harry Olsen.

pointed tips. Margins are toothed. Leafstalks are short, thin, and light green. Spring leaves have rose-tinted to pink edging which blends almost to the center. In the late spring, very tiny yellow or white specks become dusted onto the bright pale green leaf. The variegation is subtle and beautiful. Fall color is bright crimson. 'Komon nishiki' can attain up to 10 ft. (3 m) tall and lends itself to bonsai and container culture. The name means "small figures on brocade."

'Korean Gem'

Amoenum Group—green. The brilliant fall colors range from yellows to oranges, often blended with red. The shoots are dark red and especially noticeable in the fall and winter. The leaves are a bright, light green in the spring and summer. They are medium-sized and fairly deeply separated into five to seven lobes. The lobes are ovate and taper to a sharp point, with finely toothed margins. 'Korean Gem' is strong growing and hardy and forms an upright, round-headed, medium-sized to large tree up to 23 ft. (7 m) high.

'Koshibori nishiki'

Palmatum Group—variegated. The light, bright green new leaves are edged with orange and red in the spring. The sand-dusted type of variegation consists of extremely fine dots and flecks of pale cream to yellow on the green. The small leaves are divided into five long-ovate lobes with

Acer palmatum 'Koshimino'. Photo by J. D. Vertrees.

shallowly toothed margins. Shoots are crimson. Fall colors graduate through yellow into orange. This short shrub has a slightly cascading habit and makes a dense but lacy plant, reaching 8 ft. (2.5 m) or so in height. It is a desirable small landscape plant and also adapts well to container culture. The name means "young pale-spotted brocade."

'Koshimino'
Other Group—green. The leaf shape, size, color, and attachment directly to the shoot are the same as for 'Hagoromo'. However, the latter never grows as vigorously as 'Koshimino', which reaches a height of 20 ft. (6 m) relatively quickly.

'Koto hime'
Dwarf Group—green. 'Kotohime' has one of the smallest leaves among Japanese maples. The leaves are divided into five ovate lobes with bluntly tail-like tips and two tiny basal lobes. Margins are deeply toothed. The leafstalks are very short. New leaves emerge a bright rose or orange-red, heaviest on the leaf edges and shading into the light green center. Summer foliage is bright, light green. Fall colors are light yellow blended with orange. This sturdy, very dense, upright, and rounded little plant is useful in special places such as alpine gardens. It is also popular with bonsai specialists and can be trained into a very tight bun shape. The name means "little harp."

'Koto ito komachi'
Dwarf Group—green. This strapleaf is extremely dwarf and unusual. The shoots are sturdy and the leaf nodes are close together, making the foliage quite dense. The small leaves have three to five lobes, with untoothed, slightly wavy margins. The relatively long, narrow, ribbonlike leaves do not lie in the same plane. Each leaf has a different curl to the lobes. The short leafstalk is very slender. This cultivar is hardy and takes full sun. It is a marvel that it grows at all, since the leaf surface is so small it can manufacture very little food. The name can be interpreted as "old harp string" or "beautiful little girl."

Acer palmatum 'Kotohime'. Photo by J. D. Vertrees.

Acer palmatum 'Koto ito komachi'. Photo by J. D. Vertrees.

Acer palmatum 'Koto maru'. Photo by Cor van Gelderen.

Acer palmatum 'Koto-no-ito'. Photo by Peter Gregory.

'Koto maru'

Dwarf Group—green. The green-leaved equivalent of 'Beni hime', 'Koto maru' is similar in leaf shape and size and growth rate. New foliage is yellow, with bronzed edges and tips, before turning dark green. The yellow-bronze new growth overlying the dark green older foliage continues throughout the growing season. The small five-lobed leaves are fairly deeply divided with each lobe broadly ovate and irregular. Margins are toothed. As is typical of witches' brooms, the center lobe is often shortened and occasionally absent. 'Koto maru' forms a dense compact slow-growing bush. The name means "round harp."

'Koto-no-ito'

Linearilobum Group—green. This strapleaf maple has slightly broader lobes than the usual linearilobum, mixed with thin stringlike lobes. The leaves have five to seven long narrow lobes of a rich green color, gradually tapering to elongate, sharp points, and with almost smooth margins. New leaves unfold with crimson tones but soon turn green. Fall colors are various yellow tones. Although an upright-growing form, 'Koto-no-ito'

does not exceed 10 ft. (3 m) in height. The bark is a good bright green and the plant is hardy. The name means "harp strings."

'Kōya san'

Dwarf Group—green. This attractive Dutch dwarf has glossy bronze-green palmate leaves. These are mainly five-lobed with narrow ovate, deeply divided lobes and relatively large coarse irregularly toothed margins. New leaves are a bright bronze-red with yellow midveins and are produced all summer to make a pleasing contrast to the bronze-green background of older leaves. 'Kōya san' forms a small dense upright bush. The name means "wild hill or mound."

'Kurabu yama'

Matsumurae Group—green. The medium-sized leaves are seven-lobed and separated to the base. Each lobe is broadly ovate with the side lobes noticeably narrower. Margins are sharply toothed. Spring growth is reddish brown, changing in the summer to a deep, rich green, becoming yellow, orange, and crimson in the fall, making this very conspicuous. This cultivar is a vigorous grower,

Acer palmatum 'Kōya san'. Photo by Peter Gregory.

Acer palmatum
'Kurabu yama'.
Photo by J. D. Vertrees.

Acer palmatum
'Kuro hime'.
Photo by Peter Gregory.

Acer palmatum
'Lemon Lime Lace'.
Photo by Harry Olsen.

reaching 13 ft. (4 m) high and wide. It is hardy and useful in the garden for its good fall color. It was named after Mount Kurabu.

'Kuro hime'

Dwarf Group—green. This dwarf cultivar goes through a kaleidoscope of colors in the spring. The typical small five- to seven-lobed palmate leaves emerge a bright pink-red, becoming green with brown-red flushed edges before changing to a mid to dark green for the summer. Fall color is bright red. 'Kuro hime' forms a dense compact small shrub. It is well suited for small gardens and containers.

'Lemon Lime Lace'

Dissectum Group—green. The leaves of this interesting two-toned dissectum emerge a very light lemon-yellow, becoming lime-green in the summer. They create a lovely two-tone effect from early summer onwards. Fall color is orange. The size and shape of the leaves are similar to 'Green Mist'. The five- to seven-lobed deeply dissected leaves have the lobes themselves dissected almost to the midrib. The margins are edged with coarse but narrow, sharply pointed teeth. This cultivar forms a compact irregular mound with semipendulous branches. It was named for the changing leaf colors.

'Lionheart'

Dissectum Group—red. This unique semiupright cultivar is almost the red counterpart to the ever-popular green-leaved 'Seiryū'. In the spring, its foliage is similar in color to that of 'Crimson Queen'. It retains this purple-red well into summer, becoming bronzed with green undertones, and turning a deep crimson in the fall. The large seven-lobed leaves are dissected to the base, the lobes themselves deeply incised. The margins have coarse but narrow, finely pointed teeth. The red leafstalks have expanded bases. When young, the attractive deep red bark is covered in closely packed vertical glaucous striations. 'Lionheart' is a vigorous small tree attaining a height of 11–13 ft. (3.5–4 m). Like 'Seiryū', it grows upright at first, but then becomes more spreading with age. The branches grow horizontally with pendulous tips to give an attractive layered and arching effect.

Acer palmatum 'Lionheart'. Photo by Harold Greer.

Acer palmatum 'Lozita'. Photo by Harold Greer.

'Lozita'

Palmatum Group—red. The main features of this cultivar are the bright rosy-red new leaves produced all summer on the background of mahogany-red older leaves, and the stunning scarlet autumn color. The leaves tend to become bronze-green in shade. They are medium-sized with five to seven deeply divided ovate-triangular lobes. Each lobe has a tail-like tip and distinctly, evenly toothed margins. The short slender leafstalks are also purple. 'Lozita' forms a bushy upright tree, eventually reaching 13–16 ft. (4–5 m) tall. It is an ideal plant for containers which tend to keep it more compact.

'Lutescens'

Amoenum Group—green. The large seven-lobed leaves are divided about halfway to their bases. The lobes are ovate but taper to sharp points and have toothed margins. The new growth is yellowish green, changing to a rich green. The real glory is the fall color, a very rich yellow or gold. This medium-sized upright tree matures at 23 ft. (7 m) or more. It is a good companion for other orange to crimson forms in a larger planting. The name means "yellowish."

'Mai mori'

Palmatum Group—variegated. The leaves are similar in shape to 'Butterfly' but slightly larger with broader lobes. The variegation is light cream to yellow on medium green to dark gray-green and occurs in patches of various sizes and in flecks. The patches sometimes occupy one side of a lobe, causing the lobe to become sickle-shaped, or may occupy the whole leaf. The small-ish leaves are deeply divided into five to seven ovate lobes, each with a tapered tip. The margins are distinctly and regularly double-toothed. This plant forms a compact densely branched small tree, more or less as wide as tall. The name means "forest dance."

Acer palmatum 'Lutescens'. Photo by Cor van Gelderen.

Acer palmatum 'Mai mori'. Photo by Peter Gregory.

Acer palmatum 'Maiko'. Photo by J. D. Vertrees.

'Maiko'

Palmatum Group—green. The foliage of this interesting small cultivar is a yellowish green to a bright green. Fall colors are pleasing yellows of different intensities. The small to medium-sized leaves are five-lobed but decidedly non-uniform. Some lobes are narrow with deeply and irregularly toothed, even lobulate, margins. A few leaves are the typical palmate shape but with very deeply toothed margins. These extremes, plus all variations between, can occur on the same plant. The red leafstalks are short and stiff. 'Maiko' makes an upright shrub up to 10 ft. (3 m) tall. After vigorous early growth, it broadens as it matures. The name means "dancing doll."

'Mapi-no-machi hime'

Dwarf Group—green. This desirable green dwarf is similar to the popular 'Kiyohime' in growth habit, leaves, and coloring. The small palmate leaves are a lovely light yellow-green edged with pink-orange in the spring, becoming light to medium green with a darker bronze-red edging which sometimes persists through the summer. The fall color is orange-red. The five-lobed leaves are deeply divided, with the lobes spread out like a star. Each lobe is ovate with a tail-like tip and clearly double-toothed margins. The pink-red leafstalks are short and slender. This plant forms a small, round densely branched shrub, reaching 6½ ft. (2 m) tall and wide. Synonym, 'Little Princess'.

'Masu kagami'

Palmatum Group—variegated. One of the most interesting of the subtly variegated maples, 'Masu kagami' has large leaves with five to seven lobes that are separated openly and deeply. Each lobe is elongate-ovate with the tip extended to a very sharp point. The margins are prominently toothed. Early spring foliage is crimson, occasionally showing strong pink tones. These colors lessen, but the reddish shades persist along the margins into late spring. The summer leaves are green but often so heavily marked as to appear almost whitish green. The extremely fine dots of white and yellow often merge to form more solid

Acer palmatum 'Mapi-no-machi hime'. Photo by Peter Gregory.

areas of light color. This cultivar does best with light shade protection. It is a hardy, medium-growing plant which eventually makes a tall shrub 13 ft. (4 m) high.

'Masu murasaki'

Palmatum Group—red. This very intense purple-red cultivar shows best leaf color in full sun. When grown close to similar cultivars, its unique color is apparent. In full shade, the leaves have almost a black-red tone with deep green shading in the center of the lobes. The leafstalks and veins are also bright red. The medium-sized seven-lobed leaf is moderately deeply separated. Each lobe is ovate-acuminate with a long tip and toothed margins. This vigorous upright plant grows to about 23 ft. (7 m) high.

'Matsugae'

Palmatum Group—variegated. Basic leaf color is a deep, almost bluish green. The variegation is along the margins or irregular. The markings are white or cream, overlaid in the spring with a deep rose. The colors lessen somewhat in the late summer, but in the fall the deep rose color intensifies in variegated areas. The small five-lobed leaves are very irregular. The long, narrow lobes are deeply separated and terminate in slender points. Sometimes the lobes are sickle-shaped, especially when heavily variegated. The edges are deeply and non-uniformly notched and/or toothed. This cultivar is intermediate between 'Butterfly' and 'Kagiri nishiki' but has a greater color depth than the latter. The general appearance is similar to 'Kagiri nishiki', and it is a little more open and less twiggy than 'Butterfly'. 'Matsugae' grows up to 10–13 ft. (3–4 m) tall. It is a hardy plant and can take full sun. The name means "pine branch."

'Matsukaze'

Matsumurae Group—green. This cultivar with deeply cut leaves makes a handsome landscape plant. The spring color is a spectacular bronzed-red to purple-red. The bright yellow-green veins add a special effect. The medium-sized leaves develop a rich green in the summer, turning a

Acer palmatum 'Masu kagami'. Photo by J. D. Vertrees.

Acer palmatum 'Masu murasaki'. Photo by Cor van Gelderen.

Acer palmatum 'Matsugae'. Photo by Harry Olsen.

Acer palmatum 'Matsukaze'. Photo by J. D. Vertrees.

Acer palmatum 'Matsuyoi'. Photo by Cor van Gelderen.

Acer palmatum 'Matthew'. Photo by Harry Olsen.

rich carmine and crimson in the fall. They have seven long, narrow, elliptic-ovate lobes which taper to long, slender points. The margins are double-toothed. The leafstalks are long and slender. Growth habit is vigorous, and the cultivar becomes a broad shrub up to 13 ft. (4 m) or so tall,. with graceful, cascading branches. It needs space to spread in order to display its unique weeping look. The name means "wind in the pine trees."

'Matsuyoi'

Amoenum Group—green. A medium-sized tree with unusual foliage. The large leaves emerge a pale yellowish green, turning to a light, bright green in the summer. The lobes bend up or down or sometimes twist slightly. Some leaves hang down, some are flat, some are on edge, creating the effect of a wind-blown coiffure. The fall color is bright yellow-orange to deep orange. The seven lobes are long-ovate, separated halfway to the base. The edges are quite notched with fine toothing between the notches. This shorter tree tends to grow rather broad and not strongly upright, reaching 10–13 ft. (3–4 m) high. The foliage appears feathery. The name can be interpreted to mean "evening breeze."

'Matthew'

Dwarf Group—green. Originating from a witches' broom, this excellent dwarf cultivar is like the better-known 'Coonara Pygmy' in leaf size and shape and in growth habit. The green palmate leaves turn a delightful yellow to deep orange and red in the fall. The plant forms a dense round small bush up to 1½ ft. (50 cm) tall and wide. It is excellent for the rock garden, patio, and containers.

'Midori-no-teiboku'

Dwarf Group—green. This unusual dwarf dissectum is an attractive low-growing plant. It stands

Acer palmatum 'Midori-no-teiboku'. Photo by Peter Gregory.

Acer palmatum 'Mikawa yatsubusa'. Photo by J. D. Vertrees.

out for its combination of dark green lace-leaved foliage and prostrate growth, only reaching 3 ft. (1 m) tall but spreading about three times as wide. The leaves resemble those of the well-known 'Viridis' in shape and size, hence the *V* in its synonym, 'V. Corbin'. The name means "green spreading."

'Mikawa yatsubusa'

Dwarf Group—green. The leaves, which overlap each other like shingles on a roof, are a light yel-low-green in the spring and bunched up at the shoot tips, becoming a medium green in the summer. The outer leaves have very bright red tips on the fine red serrations of the margins. The leaves, slightly longer than those of other dwarf forms, have five to seven moderately deeply divided lobes. Each lobe is oblong-ovate, with a long, tapering pointed tip. The margins are finely toothed. The leaf base is straight or shallowly heart-shaped, with all the lobes point-ing forward. The growth is multibranched, re-sulting in a very dense compact little plant. The name can be translated as "a small cluster of three rivers."

'Mini Mondo'

Palmatum Group—green. This semidwarf has tiny green leaves with five to seven lobes. Fall color is deep red. The leaves are similar in shape and size to those of the dwarf 'Hanami nishiki'; however, 'Mini Mondo' grows twice as tall, reaching 6½ ft. (2 m) high in 10 years, and forms a small compact rounded shrub. Some sources believe 'Tiny Leaf' may be identical. The name means "small world."

'Mirte'

Matsumurae Group—green. Spring leaves are mid chocolate-brown with light green veining and covered with a soft pubescence. They be-come an unusual dark olive-green by early sum-mer and then turn bronze-green. Fall color is or-ange-yellow. The current shoots are covered in a gray bloom. The large leaves have seven to nine deeply incised ovate lobes with tail-like pointed tips. The margins have conspicuous, sharply pointed, hooked teeth. This strong-growing up-right cultivar reaches up to 26 ft. (8 m) tall and wide. It was named after a granddaughter of Dutch nurseryman D. M. van Gelderen.

'Mizu kuguri'

Amoenum Group—green. The spring color is un-usual—a light green background with a pinkish-rose to a light brick-red overshading. Summer color is a deeper green. The medium-sized leaves

Acer palmatum 'Mini Mondo'. Photo by Harold Greer.

Acer palmatum 'Mirte'. Photo by Cor van Gelderen.

Acer palmatum
'Mizu kuguri'.
Photo by Cor van
Gelderen.

Acer palmatum
'Momoiro kōya
san'. Photo by
Peter Gregory.

are seven-lobed with a flat base. The ovate lobes taper to elongated, narrow tips and have fine sharp-toothed margins. This cultivar becomes a bushy plant, reaching 10 ft. (3 m) high. The name may be translated as "passing under a waterfall or fountain."

'Momoiro kōya san'

Palmatum Group—red. This small-leaved compact red cultivar from the Netherlands has attractive color changes through the season. Some of the five- to seven-lobed palmate leaves may have a light creamy variegation. The new spring leaves are a lovely peach color, changing slowly to orange-red, then red for the summer, and becoming bronze-green by late summer, before turning red in the fall. This small tree is similar in shape and size to 'Seigen' but needs light shade. It is ideal for bonsai and container culture. The name means "peach-colored Mount Koya."

Acer palmatum
'Mon Papa'. Photo
by Peter Gregory.

Acer palmatum
'Moonfire'. Photo
by J. D. Vertrees.

'Mon Papa'

Matsumurae Group—red. Similar in leaf to 'Nicholsonii' and 'Matsukaze', this small Belgium cultivar has outstanding fall color. The medium-sized to large leaves are deeply divided into seven long-ovate sharply pointed lobes with regular, narrow, sharply pointed teeth which give the foliage an attractive feathery appearance. The purple-red leaves become bronze-green by late summer before turning a brilliant orange-red in the fall. This maple forms a wide-spreading tree up to 13 ft. (4 m) tall. The name means "my papa."

'Moonfire'

Matsumurae Group—red. The excellent purple-red to black-red color is almost opalescent. Diffused sun gives it a faint blue overtone similar to that of 'Nuresagi'. The good deep colors last very well throughout summer. Fall color is a delightful crimson. The large deeply divided leaves have

Acer palmatum 'Murakumo'. Photo by Robert Jamgochian.

Acer palmatum 'Murasaki kiyohime'. Photo by Daniel Otis.

elongate-ovate lobes, gradually tapering to fine points and with finely toothed margins. The red leafstalks are short. This cultivar assumes an upright, rounded canopy, reaching about 23 ft. (7 m) tall. It is very worthwhile for the landscape. The durable, long-lasting season of color rivals that of the well-known 'Bloodgood'.

'Murakumo'

Palmatum Group—green. The medium-sized leaves are usually seven-lobed and deeply divided. The ovate-elongate lobes are wide in the center and come to a strong point. The margins are finely toothed. Spring color is almost crimson and soon becomes a very good, deep purple-red. Fall color is crimson. This upright cultivar is quite hardy and reaches about 20 ft. (6 m) tall at maturity. It is valuable in the garden landscape because it retains the red colors well into late summer. The name probably means "cluster of clouds" or "village in the clouds," and is sometimes spelled 'Muragumo'.

'Murasaki kiyohime'

Dwarf Group—green. The small deeply divided, five-lobed leaves radiate openly from the center. Each lobe is ovate-lanceolate, tapering to an elongated, sharp tip. The center lobe is very prominent. Spring foliage has a broad edging of bright purple-red, merging gradually into the yellow-green center. The leaves change to a solid green in the summer. Fall colors are gold or orange blends. This desirable dwarf cultivar is hardy but not a vigorous grower. It is excellent for alpine plantings, container culture, and bonsai. It tends to be upright, reaching 3 ft. (1 m) tall. The name means "purple and yellow dwarf," referring to the spring leaf color and plant habit.

'Mure hibari'

Matsumurae Group—green. Beautiful though little known, 'Mure hibari' has small leaves which are very deeply divided into seven lobes. The lobes in turn are narrow, elongate-lanceolate, tapering to long, slender points, and radiating

Acer palmatum 'Mure hibari'. Photo by J. D. Vertrees.

Acer palmatum 'Muro gawa'. Photo by Cor van Gelderen.

sharply outwards. The margins are slightly trough-shaped and prominently toothed. Spring leaves are light green with bright brick-red margins, becoming entirely green in the summer. Fall color is yellow to crimson. This medium-strong grower forms an upright plant up to 16 ft. (5 m) tall. It is quite vigorous and hardy. The name means "flock of skylarks."

'Muro gawa'

Amoenum Group—red. This strong cultivar brings a lot of color to the garden. In the spring and early summer it is a striking orange-red with contrasting green veins. As the season progresses, the tones change to rusty green, then to a deep bronze-green by late summer. Fall colors are orange-reds to crimson. The large moderately deeply divided leaves have seven to nine lobes which are long-ovate, each tapering to a slender point. The margins are toothed. The green leafstalks are long and slender. 'Muro

gawa' is hardy and fairly vigorous, becoming round-topped with pendulous outer branches, and growing to 20 ft. (6 m) tall with a spread of 10–13 ft. (3–4 m). It is named after the Muro River in central Japan.

'Musashino'

Matsumurae Group—red. The leaf color is a deep purple-red. As the new leaf develops, the surface is covered with a minute, light pubescence, bringing out the rich purple tones. This pubescence disappears, but the rich color persists all summer. Fall color is a brilliant crimson hue. The large leaves have five to seven very deeply divided lobes, each one elongate-ovate, terminating in a long, narrow, tapering point. The margins are sharply toothed. Fast-growing, this strongly upright cultivar has a rounded crown and matures at 23–26 ft. (7-8 m) tall. It is hardy and suitable for cooler areas. The name is after a suburb of Tokyo. Synonym, 'Nomura'.

Acer palmatum 'Musashino'. Photo by J. D. Vertrees.

Acer palmatum 'Nanese gawa'. Photo by J. D. Vertrees.

'Nanese gawa'

Amoenum Group—green. The medium-sized leaves have five to seven deeply divided lobes which are ovate and terminate in long, narrow sharp points. Margins are toothed. The basal lobes point outward to form a flat leaf base. Leaf color is crimson to purplish red with contrasting green veins in the spring, becoming entirely green in the summer, and turning bright crimson in the fall. This cultivar reaches 13 ft. (4 m) tall and forms a spreading bush. It may be named after the Nanese River, the location of which remains a mystery.

'Nicholsonii'

Matsumurae Group—green. The best feature of this very old cultivar is the golden-yellow to crimson fall color of the leaves. Spring foliage is a good red, slightly purplish, becoming a deep, rich green

Acer palmatum 'Nicholsonii'. Photo by J. D. Vertrees.

in the summer. The medium-sized deeply divided leaves are seven-lobed, each lobe elongate-ovate and ending in a fine point. Margins are sharply toothed. 'Nicholsonii' is a medium-strong grower reaching 16 ft. (5 m) high and wide.

'Nigrum'

Palmatum Group—red. The foliage is a rich purple-red to almost black-red. Young leaves have a characteristic fine silvery white pubescence . The leaf color becomes brown-green in late summer. Fall colors are bright red and crimson. The medium-sized leaves have seven ovate-acuminate lobes, each ending with a sharp tip, and with toothed margins. This cultivar grows rapidly when young, later slows down to reach 13–16 ft. (4–5 m) tall. The name means "black," referring to the leaf color.

'Nishiki gasane'

Palmatum Group—variegated. The starlike variegation is almost unique. The deep green leaf is

Acer palmatum 'Nigrum'. Photo by Cor van Gelderen.

Acer palmatum 'Nishiki gasane'. Photo by J. D. Vertrees.

speckled and flecked with gold which is often concentrated around the margins. In the spring, the heavily variegated leaves have apricot-colored shading from the edges towards the center, becoming clear gold variegations on a green background in the summer. The medium-sized leaves have five to seven moderately deeply divided ovate lobes, terminating in long, slender tips. The margins are coarsely toothed. This upright-growing small tree matures up to 10 ft. (3 m) high and needs protection from hot afternoon sun. It is almost identical with 'Sagara nishiki'. The name means "overlapping variegations."

'Nishiki gawa'
Pine-bark maple

Palmatum Group—green. The rough pinelike bark is the outstanding feature here. The older the plant, the rougher the bark, becoming corky with coarse, longitudinal, irregular convoluted creases. This characteristic begins to develop when the plant is two or three years old. The small moderately deeply divided leaves usually have seven elongate-ovate lobes tapering to long

Acer palmatum 'Nishiki gawa'. Photo by J. D. Vertrees.

Acer palmatum 'Nishiki momiji'.
Photo by Ray Prag.

Acer palmatum 'Novum'.
Photo by J. D. Vertrees.

points. The margins are strongly toothed. Spring color is light green edged with a light shading of red. Summer leaves are bright green, turning a strong yellow in the fall. This upright, bushy tree grows to 20 ft. (6 m) tall. It is popular for bonsai culture.

'Nishiki momiji'

Matsumurae Group—green. The spring leaves unfold with a pinkish or orange-red tone which persists along the margins as the leaves mature and turn to light green. Fall color is an especially brilliant display of crimson to fire-red. The medium-sized leaves have five to seven moderately deeply divided long, slender, lanceolate lobes gradually tapering to sharp points. The margins are double-toothed. This upright maple

with a spreading crown grows to a height of up to 16 ft. (5 m).

'Novum'

Amoenum Group—red. The medium-sized to large leaves have five to seven ovate lobes which taper to slender, sharp points and are divided at least halfway to the base. The spring and early summer color is a light purple-red, not as dark as in 'Bloodgood' or 'Nuresagi'. The leaves are a bright, almost orange-red in midsummer, becoming green-red in late summer. Fall color is an intense scarlet. This strong, upright-growing maple can reach more than 23 ft. (7 m) high. It forms a round-topped small tree which is hardy and vigorous. The name means "new." Synonym, 'Atropurpureum Novum'.

Acer palmatum 'Nuresagi'.
Photo by J. D. Vertrees.

Acer palmatum 'Ō kagami'.
Photo by Cor van Gelderen.

'Nuresagi'

Matsumurae Group—red. This excellent purple cultivar has large leaves with five to seven lobes which radiate strongly outward. Each lobe is oblong-ovate, ending in a long, slender tip. The lobes are deeply divided, so the foliage appears quite lacy. The stiff leafstalks are bright red. The deep, rich, dark purple-red leaf color is unusual. In the spring and early summer, the leaves appear to have an opalescence, even a bluish overtone, in a certain light. They retain the dark purple-red tones into late summer, occasionally becoming suffused with a slight, deep green mottling. The twigs and branches are a deep maroon color with a grayish tone caused by fine whitish vertical striations which are a pleasant feature. This very hardy cultivar is upright and vigorous, and needs space to spread. It may reach 16–20 ft. (5–6 m) tall. The name means "wet heron."

'Ō kagami'

Palmatum Group—red. The beautiful purplish red of the new foliage deepens into a shiny blackish red in the summer. The strong color lasts until late summer when green tones blend in. Fall colors are red and scarlet. The large leaves have five to seven lobes which radiate markedly, with the two basal lobes overlapping the leafstalk like a fully extended fan. The lobes are broadly ovate and moderately deeply separated. The margins are uniformly toothed. This desirable color form makes a delightful upright small tree to about 16 ft. (5 m) tall at maturity. The name means "mirror" and probably refers to the shiny summer leaf color.

Acer palmatum 'Octopus'. Photo by Peter Gregory.

'Octopus'

Dissectum Group—red. The vigorous long new shoots or "tentacles" of this attractive red dissectum arch outward and downward to give it its name. The new leaves are pink-red with narrow greenish midribs, becoming a darker plum-red, then coppery red with a greenish tinge along the midribs in the summer. The fall color is bright crimson-red. The medium-sized leaves have deeply dissected lobes with sharply pointed teeth on the margins. The slender leafstalks are orange-red. This strong-growing plant forms a broad irregular dome, reaching about 10–13 ft. (3–4 m) high and 10–11 ft. (3–3.5 m) wide.

'Ogino nagare'

Palmatum Group—green. New leaves are light yellow with a rose tint along the margins. Summer foliage is light green with indistinct subdued flecks of lighter green scattered over the leaves and occasional pale cream or white spots. Fall colors are yellow and deep gold. The medium-sized leaves have five ovate-acuminate moderately deeply separated lobes which radiate outward. Margins are toothed and feathery. This strong-growing small tree is delicate looking but hardy. It may reach 16 ft. (5 m) or more high. The name means "fan stream," possibly referring to the Kyoto festival in which members of the ruling class tossed beautiful fans into a stream which were then collected by commoners.

'Ogon sarasa'

Matsumurae Group—red. The color combination and leaf shape identify this interesting plant. Spring leaves are brick-red brushed over a deep green background, with contrasting light green midribs. Each leaf varies in intensity. In late summer, the leaves become a bronze-green. Fall colors are bright orange and crimson. Each medium-sized leaf is deeply divided into seven elongate-elliptical lobes which gradually taper to narrow

Acer palmatum 'Ogino nagare'. Photo by J. D. Vertrees.

Acer palmatum 'Ogon sarasa'. Photo by Cor van Gelderen.

Acer palmatum 'Ōjishi'. Photo by J. D. Vertrees.

Acer palmatum 'Okukuji nishiki'. Photo by J. D. Vertrees.

points. The lobe sides are curved upward, creating a shallow trough. This plant forms a tall shrub up to 23 ft. (7 m) tall and 10 ft. (3 m) wide. The name means "gold calico cloth."

'Ōjishi'

Dwarf Group—green. 'Ōjishi', meaning "male lion," is smaller and more compact than 'Mejishi', meaning "female lion," which is better known as the popular 'Shishigashira'. It has similar but larger, bright green, less crinkly leaves which turn a bright gold in the fall. The leaves are more closely arranged on the stem. The rate of growth is slow, making a very dwarf, multibranched, little shrub which grows up to 6½ ft. (2 m) high.

'Okukuji nishiki'

Palmatum Group—variegated. This semidwarf tree with highly variegated foliage resembles a smaller compact form of the better-known 'Butterfly'. The small five-lobed leaves vary in shape. Colors are white to cream on a base of powdery green. New leaves may have a tinge of pink on the edges. Sometimes entire leaves are white or cream. Fall color is rose-pink on the whitish areas. The leafstalks are very thin and short. The tree or tall shrub is upright and dense but not a strong grower. Its lightly colored leaves make it a good companion plant for the dark green of evergreen plants.

'Okushimo'

Palmatum Group—green. The outstanding features of this maple include odd-shaped leaves, sweeping upright growth, and beautiful gold fall color which seems almost fluorescent at times. The summer foliage is a rich green. The small leaves have five to seven lobes which are moderately deeply separated and radiating stiffly outward. Each lobe is lanceolate and tapers to a sharp stiff point. Intriguingly, the slightly bluntly notched lobe margins roll upward, almost forming a tapering tube. The lobe tips bend upward. The stiff leafstalks are pink-red and the shoots green. This stiffly upright, vase-shaped tree is vigorous, often reaching 26 ft. (8 m) or more. It is

Acer palmatum 'Okushimo'. Photo by J. D. Vertrees.

very desirable for landscaping, and its compact habit adapts it to bonsai.

'Kurui jishi' is similar to 'Okushimo' but with smaller leaves and habit, only reaching 6½ ft. (2 m) high. The name can be interpreted as "a confused lion."

'Ōmato'

Amoenum Group—green. Like 'Ōsakazuki', 'Ōmato' has large leaves. The leaves have five to seven ovate lobes which gradually taper to sharp points. Margins are sharply toothed. Spring leaves may have a tinge of orange-red but soon take on a rich green color and are resistant to

Acer palmatum 'Ōmato'. Photo by Harold Greer.

sunburn. Fall color is a rich red. This strong-growing, round-headed tree reaches up to 26 ft. (8 m) tall and almost as wide. The name means "large target," referring to the leaves.

'Omure yama'

Matsumurae Group—green. As the height of this excellent cascading cultivar increases, the pendulous branches become willowy and form a long curtain around the outside. The medium-sized very deeply divided leaves have seven long, slender lobes with deeply toothed margins. The green spring leaves have bright orange edges, soon becoming a uniform brilliant green for summer. Fall colors are a spectacular gold and crimson. Young plants are vigorous and upright, later showing the pendulous character and becoming rounded with long cascading side branches. The tree reaches up to 16 ft. (5 m) tall with a spread of 13–16 ft. (4–5 m). It is named after Mount Omure.

'Orange Dream'

Palmatum Group—green. Selected for its refreshing spring-colored foliage, this lovely cultivar produces dark orange leaves which quickly become lemon-yellow with orange-tinged margins and tips. 'Orange Dream' is similar to the popular

Acer palmatum 'Omure yama'. Photo by J. D. Vertrees.

'Katsura', but the leaves appear later, so are less likely to be damaged by early spring cold spells, and they retain their bright yellow for much longer, changing slowly to light green in the summer. Fall color is yellow-gold. The small to medium-sized leaves are moderately deeply di-vided into seven lobes. Slightly broader than long, the ovate lobes have short tail-like pointed tips with coarsely toothed margins. The red-tinged leafstalks are stiff. This desirable cultivar becomes an upright bushy shrub, reaching 10–13 ft. (3–4 m) tall. Like most cultivars with light-colored leaves, it is best in partial shade.

Acer palmatum 'Orange Dream'. Photo by Peter Gregory.

'Orangeola'

Dissectum Group—red. 'Orangeola' is noted for the bright orange-red spring foliage. The leaves turn a rich red-green, still with an orange flush, throughout the summer, boosted by a second flush of orange-red leaves in midsummer, then becoming dark red before turning fiery orange-red in the fall. The large five- to seven-lobed leaves are deeply divided to the base, and each lobe is itself deeply incised. The red leafstalks are short and slender. Although vigorous growing, this cultivar is one of the smaller dissectums, barely more than 10 ft. (3 m) high when fully

Acer palmatum 'Orangeola'. Photo by Cor van Gelderen.

grown. It forms an attractive cascading mound, usually taller than wide.

'Oregon Sunset'

Matsumurae Group—red. This cultivar has graceful, colorful foliage and forms a small neat, compact, rounded bush. It has outstanding spring and fall colors. The leaves emerge a soft red, quickly becoming plum-red and, in the fall, turning a vivid sunset-red. The largish leaves are deeply divided into five to seven elongate-ovate lobes, each with a long, slender tip. The margins have numerous fine, narrow-pointed teeth. The lobe tips tend to curve downwards slightly like a relaxed hand. 'Oregon Sunset' is a good small tree for limited space whether in the smaller landscape or in containers.

'Oridono nishiki'

Palmatum Group—variegated. The medium-sized leaves are moderately deeply divided into five to seven separated lobes, each with a long, tapering point and toothed margins. The leafstalks are pink and slender. The base leaf color is a rich, deep green which holds well until the fall. Spring foliage is bright pink, white, cream, or any combination of these, with various-sized areas of green. Sometimes new leaves are entirely white or pink. Strongly variegated leaf portions will curve or be sickle-shaped. New shoots are sometimes pink or pink-striped, which distinguishes this cultivar from the similar 'Asahi zuru'. The variegation is more reliable than that of many variegated maples. 'Oridono nishiki' is sturdy and vigorous, forming an upright, round-topped tree of 16–20 ft. (5–6 m) in 15–20 years. It is among the best cultivars in its group. The name means "richly colored fabric of the master."

'Karasu gawa' is similar to 'Oridono nishiki' but the light bright pink new growth is more spectacular, and some leaves retain streaks of light pink in the white variegation throughout

Acer palmatum 'Oregon Sunset'. Photo by Cor van Gelderen.

Acer palmatum 'Oridono nishiki'. Photo by Peter Gregory.

Acer palmatum 'Ornatum'. Photo by J. D. Vertrees.

the summer. The growth habit is narrow and upright, broadening with age and attaining 13 ft. (4 m) or so high. This maple is not a vigorous grower and should have a protected spot in the garden and also protection from strong sun. The name means "crow river."

'Ornatum'

Dissectum Group—red. The interesting spring and early summer foliage is more bronze-red than that of other red dissectums, such as 'Crimson Queen' or 'Inaba shidare'. In the late summer, it becomes greenish bronze, turning crimson-red in the fall. The large leaves have seven long, narrow lobes, each with deeply dissected side lobes which are themselves deeply toothed. Plants may reach 10 ft. (3 m) or more high but create a mounded shape with a spread of 10–13 ft. (3–4 m). This very old cultivar from Europe has been popular because of its reliability and distinctive foliage color. It is hardy and makes a good color contrast in the landscape.

'**Brocade**' is similar to 'Ornatum' but with the red being a soft deep color that holds well into summer, then gradually turns to a green-red and bronze.

'Ōsakazuki'

Amoenum Group—green. The intense crimson fall color makes this a favorite cultivar in the garden. The large leaves have seven broadly ovate lobes, each ending in a narrow tip. The lobes are separated halfway to the base and have uniformly toothed margins. Sometimes the leaves "cup" at the base. Leaf color is a good rich green. Fall color is likened to a burning bush—an intense crimson which, even at dusk, seems to glow. This sturdy, hardy cultivar forms a round-topped, small tree not exceeding 26 ft. (8 m) tall. The name means "leaf like a saki cup."

'Oshio beni'

Amoenum Group—red. New growth is orange-red becoming bronzed, then reddish green. It does not retain the bright colors as well as 'Bloodgood', 'Moonfire', or 'Nuresagi', and tends

Acer palmatum 'Ōsakazuki'. Photo by J. D. Vertrees.

Acer palmatum 'Oshio beni'. Photo by Peter Gregory.

Acer palmatum 'Ōshū shidare'. Photo by J. D. Vertrees.

Acer palmatum 'Otohime'. Photo by Peter Gregory.

Acer palmatum 'Otome zakura'. Photo by Cor van Gelderen.

to burn in hot sun. Fall color is a bright scarlet. The large leaves have seven broadly ovate lobes terminating in long, sharp points and divided halfway to the base. The margins are finely toothed. This sturdy upright-grower matures at 20–26 ft. (6–8 m) high and has a spreading canopy. It is a good companion tree for color contrast. The name means "large red tide."

'Ōshū shidare'

Matsumurae Group—red. This famous cultivar has long been a favorite in Japan and is the red equivalent of the green-leaved 'Omure yama'. The leaves are intermediate between the Matsumurae and Dissectum Groups. The foliage is a strong purple-red or maroon in the spring and summer, becoming a strong crimson in the fall. The medium-sized leaves have lobes which radiate markedly and are separated almost entirely to the base. Each is elongate-lanceolate, narrow at the base, and tapering to a long, slender tip. The margins are finely toothed. This attractive small, round-headed tree has a cascading form, the pendulous branches descending gracefully to the ground. Mature trees reach up to 16 ft. (5 m) high and wide.

'Otohime'

Dwarf Group—green. The spring leaves of this strong dwarf are a bright, lively yellow-green with narrow reddish edging and tips, a color maintained throughout the summer. Fall colors are a pleasant yellow to orange. The small leaves have five moderately deeply divided lobes which radiate out like a star. Each lobe is ovate-triangular and tapers to a sharp point. The margins are uniformly and finely toothed. The leafstalks are long and thin. This shrub is tight and dense, becoming flat-topped and broader than high. A 10-year-old plant reached almost 28 in. (70 cm) tall and 4 ft. (1.3 m) wide. 'Otohime' lends itself to bonsai culture and may be named after Queen Otohime who, according to a Japanese fable, reigned at the bottom of an ocean kingdom.

Acer palmatum 'Palmatifidum'. Photo by J. D. Vertrees.

'Otome zakura'

Palmatum Group—green. The small dense bushy tree produces two kinds of brilliant spring leaves on the same plant. The larger leaves form on new vigorous shoots and are moderately deeply separated into five to seven lobes which strongly radiate outward. Each lobe is ovate with a long, sharp point and lightly toothed margins. The small leaves on older wood and less vigorous shoots have long, narrow lobes with almost parallel sides. The margins are shallowly notched. Leaf color is a striking bright orange to pink-flame in the spring, changing to maroon then greenish hues in the summer. This cultivar is very outstanding and attractive. The name means "maiden cherry," referring to the spring color.

'Palmatifidum'

Dissectum Group—green. The large rich green leaves have seven long, narrow, incised lobes separated entirely to the base. The foliage turns yellow, gold, and orange in the fall, making a very colorful display. The growth is sturdy, durable, hardy, and strongly cascading. 'Palmatifidum' makes a beautiful mound-shaped plant. Older plants are often wider than they are tall, up to 10 ft. (3 m) high and more than 13 ft. (4 m) wide. The name means "palmate-shaped."

Acer palmatum
'Peaches and Cream'.
Photo by Peter
Gregory.

Acer palmatum
'Pendulum Julian'.
Photo by Harold
Greer.

'Inaba shidare' is the red counterpart of 'Palmatifidum'. The name means "cascading ricelike leaf."

'Peaches and Cream'

Matsumurae Group—variegated. The spring foliage emerges a cream to greenish cream with a soft rose-red around the edges. The veins are conspicuous and of a contrasting deep green. Fall color ranges from yellow to buff with darker tips. The medium-sized leaves are deeply divided into five to seven ovate lobes with tapered, sharply pointed tips. The margins are very coarsely toothed. The teeth have sharp tips pointing in various directions, causing the margins to look like a prickly holly leaf. The green leafstalks are short and stout, and the slender shoots are a light green. This pretty but delicate selection forms a small tree or shrub about 10 ft. (3 m) high and wide.

'Pendulum Julian'

Dissectum Group—red. The large seven-lobed leaves are a bronze-green in the spring with green veining, becoming deep purple-red in the summer and rusty green with a reddish undertone later. Fall color is a vivid crimson-orange. This plant is quite pendulous and wide-spreading, and young plants must be staked early to reach the required height. 'Pendulum Julian' is very hardy. Older plants have survived 0°F (−18°C) and heavy coverings of ice.

'Pink Filigree'

Dissectum Group—red. This cross between 'Ornatum' and 'Stella Rossa' has unusual spring color and delightful summer color. Spring leaves are a unique rose-pink with conspicuous yellow veins, becoming purple-red which makes a pleasing background to the bright rose new foliage

Acer palmatum 'Pink Filigree'. Photo by Cor van Gelderen.

appearing throughout the summer. Leaf coloring is at its best in full sun. Fall color is orange-red. The medium-sized leaves are similar in shape and size to those of 'Stella Rossa'. The five to seven lobes are deeply divided to the base. Each lobe is itself divided into sharply toothed sublobes. The new vigorous shoots grow upward and outward, producing a broad cascading mound, similar in shape and size to 'Ornatum', reaching about 10 ft. (3 m) tall.

'Pixie'

Dwarf Group—red. This cultivar, a possible sport from 'Bloodgood', is similar but for the shorter growth and more deeply cut lobes. New leaves are a bright pink-red, becoming deep red in the summer and turning a fiery scarlet in the fall. The leaves are deeply divided into five to seven widely spreading, broadly ovate lobes with long, pointed tips. The margins are coarsely but regularly toothed. The pink leafstalk is slender and stiff. 'Pixie' forms a dense round-topped bush up to 6½ ft. (2 m) tall and wide.

The similar **'Skeeter's Broom'** also arose as a witches' broom from 'Bloodgood' but has slightly longer lobes. Any lobe, not only the center lobe, may be short and rounded.

'Purple Ghost'

Matsumurae Group—variegated. Purple netting characterizes this exciting introduction, one of the Ghost series from Oregon. The stunning

Acer palmatum 'Pixie'. Photo by Peter Gregory.

Acer palmatum 'Purple Ghost'. Photo by Talon Buchholz.

spring leaves are a deep red with an even deeper purple-red network of veins. The summer color is red with dark purple-red veining and margins. The leaves turn a fiery orange and scarlet in the fall. The large seven-lobed deeply divided leaves have distinctly sharp-toothed and attractively crumpled margins. This semiupright rounded tree, estimated to reach about 10–12 ft. (3–3.9 m) tall and 5 ft. (1.5 m) wide, makes a dramatic contrast or focal point in the garden landscape.

'Purpureum'

Amoenum Group—red. This old British cultivar has medium-sized leaves, which are a deep purple-red in the spring and early summer, becoming a bronze-green in late summer, then turning a bright scarlet in the fall. The leaves are moderately deeply divided into seven ovate lobes with pointed tips and evenly toothed margins. The small basal lobes are held at right angles to the leafstalks. 'Purpureum' is slow-growing and upright with a dense round-headed crown. It reaches 16 ft. (5 m) high and wide. The name means "purple."

'Red Autumn Lace'

Dissectum Group—green. This outstanding dissectum is noted for the bright green summer foliage with reddish bronze new leaves at the shoot tips. The fall color is special, changing through yellow to orange to a vivid red. The large leaves are deeply divided into seven lobes, with the lobes themselves divided into coarsely toothed

Acer palmatum 'Purpureum'. Photo by Cor van Gelderen.

Acer palmatum 'Red Autumn Lace'. Photo by Cor van Gelderen.

Acer palmatum 'Red Cloud'. Photo by Cor van Gelderen.

Acer palmatum 'Red Dragon'. Photo by Peter Gregory.

sublobes. This cultivar forms a broad cascading mound up to 10–13 ft. (3–4 m) tall with a spread of 13–16 ft. (4–5 m).

'Red Cloud'

Linearilobum Group—red. This red strapleaf from Oregon has bright red new leaves in the spring, changing to purple-red which lasts all summer, until turning an eye-catching orange-red in the autumn. 'Red Cloud' eventually forms a rounded tree of about 10–13 ft. (3–4 m) tall, more open and wide-spreading than most strapleaves. This habit, combined with the long narrow five- to seven-lobed leaves, gives a cloudlike effect, hence the name.

'Red Dragon'

Dissectum Group—red. This purple-red dissectum keeps its deep color in sun or shade better than any other red dissectum. Spring leaves are bright scarlet, becoming dark burgundy in the summer, and turning an outstanding flaming scarlet in the fall. The large leaves are deeply cut into seven lobes, the lobes themselves deeply

incised. Margins have coarse, sharply pointed, and hooked teeth. The slender leafstalks are purple. Growth habit is like a dwarf form of 'Crimson Queen' and forms a compact well-branched cascading mound, reaching 8 ft. (2.5 m) high. 'Red Dragon' needs protection from cold wind and summer drought, but makes an excellent small garden, rock garden, container, or bonsai plant.

'Red Filigree Lace'

Dissectum Group—red. Among the most beautiful and unusual of dissectums, this selection has leaves that must be seen to be appreciated. They are among the most finely cut of the laceleaf types. The color is a deep purple-red or maroon all summer, turning bright crimson in the fall. The medium-sized leaves are seven-lobed. The very slender lobes are deeply cut to the midrib, with the dissected side portions equally fine and edged with sharp fine teeth. This gives a filigree-like look to the foliage, and the overall effect is one of extreme beauty. The rate of growth is not as fast as in most dissectums.

Acer palmatum 'Red Filigree Lace'. Photo by Peter Gregory.

Acer palmatum 'Red Flash'. Photo by Cor van Gelderen.

Acer palmatum 'Red Pygmy'. Photo by Cor van Gelderen.

Acer palmatum 'Red Spider'. Photo by Harold Greer.

'Red Flash'

Matsumurae Group—red. The vivid red spring foliage becomes dark purple-red, holding its color well throughout the summer, especially in full sun. In late summer, the leaves become green-hued. The vivid red new leaves appearing during the summer contrast well with the darker red background of older leaves. The medium-sized five- to seven-lobed leaves are moderately deeply divided, with each ovate lobe having a pointed tip and toothed margins. This moderately strong grower only reaches 13–16 ft. (4–5 m) high so is suitable for smaller gardens. It is often multistemmed and forms a medium-sized upright bush or tree.

Acer palmatum 'Red Spray'. Photo by Peter Gregory.

'Red Pygmy'

Linearilobum Group—red. This excellent red cultivar has large five- to seven-lobed lacy red or bright red-maroon leaves, with the long, thin, and straplike lobes separated entirely to the base. The color, which becomes more purplish in late summer, holds much better and sunburns less than that of 'Atrolineare'. 'Red Pygmy' becomes round-topped and is smaller and less upright or rangy than other linearilobums. It reaches 8 ft. (2.5 m) high and 5–6½ ft. (1.5–2 m) wide. This cultivar makes a delightful contrast in shape and tone when combined with other forms.

'Red Spider'

Linearilobum Group—red. The leaves of this Canadian selection are remarkably uniform in shape, size, and color. They are an even red which lasts into the fall, when the color turns a vibrant sanguine-red. The medium-sized leaves are divided into five straplike lobes, with the two basal lobes stretched outward to form a flat leaf base or angled slightly forward. The long-ovate lobes are chunkier than those of most strap-leaves and have numerous fine sharp-tipped teeth along the margins. 'Red Spider' forms an upright small tree, reaching 13 ft. (4 m) high, with horizontal branches whose tips tend to curve down to give a graceful lacy effect.

'Red Spray'

Amoenum Group—red. Similar in leaf, color, and growth habit to the well-known 'Bloodgood', 'Red Spray' is said to be even more vigorous. The large five- to seven-lobed leaves are divided about halfway to the base, each lobe broadly ovate with finely toothed margins. Spring leaves are a bright pink-red, darkening to purple-red in the summer and turning a fiery orange-red in the fall. This cultivar grows into an upright broad-topped tree, up to 39 ft. (12 m) tall.

Acer palmatum 'Red Wood'. Photo by Harold Greer.

Acer palmatum 'Royle'. Photo by Peter Gregory.

'Red Wood'

Palmatum Group—green. Colorful winter bark distinguishes this Oregon cultivar. The coral-red shoots are similar to those of the popular 'Sango kaku' and hold their color for two years. The small-ish five- to seven-lobed leaves are a light yellow-green in the spring, becoming a fresh green for summer, then turning golden-yellow with pink and red tinges in the fall. 'Red Wood' forms an up-right tree, reaching up to 13 ft. (4 m) tall. It makes an excellent landscape and container plant.

'Royle'

Dwarf Group—red. Originating as a witches' broom on *Acer palmatum* f. *atropurpureum* in New Jersey, 'Royle' has small irregularly shaped leaves which are divided into five to seven lobes and bunched together. This dwarf forms a small rounded ball which eventually reaches 5 ft. (1.5 m) tall. The autumn color is a brilliant crimson. Synonym, 'Royal'.

Acer palmatum 'Rubrum'. Photo by J. D. Vertrees.

'Rubrum'

Amoenum Group—red. The seven ovate lobes of this large-leaved cultivar are separated over halfway to the base. The lobes taper to sharp points and have slightly toothed margins. The color is lighter in early spring, becoming a rich, dark maroon-red in late spring and green-red or bronze in the summer. Fall color is a strong crim-

Acer palmatum 'Ryūzu'. Photo by Peter Gregory.

Acer palmatum 'Sagara nishiki'. Photo by Peter Gregory.

Acer palmatum 'Sango kaku'. Photo by J. D. Vertrees.

son. This hardy, strong-growing, upright tree has a broadly spreading crown as it matures. It reaches 13 ft. (4 m) high and is even wider than high. The name means "red."

'Ryūzu'

Dwarf Group—green. This delightful dwarf has tightly spaced, overlapping, and bunched leaves. In the spring, the leaves have faint pink to deep orange shades on a pale green background, becoming green in the summer. The margins are very prominently toothed, the teeth bright brick-red. The foliage turns a stunning fall color of warm orange-yellow. The small leaves have five to seven ovate lobes tapering to long, sharp points. The lobe edges bend slightly up, almost making a shallow trough. This compact little

shrub is popular for bonsai or the rock garden. It grows into a flattened globe shape and reaches little more than 6½ ft. (2 m) high. The name means "ornamental dragon's head," referring to the bunched leaves.

'Sagara nishiki'

Palmatum Group—variegated. Pale yellow variegations on light green foliage make this a beautiful cultivar. In the spring, the new leaves have an overshading of pink on the yellow margins. The small to medium-sized leaves are moderately deeply divided into five broadly ovate lobes with slender tips and double-toothed margins. 'Sagara nishiki' forms a compact shrub or small tree up to 6½–10 ft. (2–3 m) tall. It needs semishade to protect the beautiful variegations

Acer palmatum 'Saoshika'. Photo by Peter Gregory.

during summer. The plant size, shape, and growth rate as well as leaf variegation are the same as 'Nishiki gasane'.

'Sango kaku'

Palmatum Group—green. 'Sango kaku' is noted for its coral bark with brilliant tones which intensify as winter approaches. The color is especially intense in snow. The small leaf has five to seven ovate-acuminate lobes which taper to sharp points. The margins are toothed. Leaf color is a bright green. The edges of new leaves have a strong reddish tinge, giving a striking appearance in the spring. In the summer, the foliage becomes a lighter green, changing to yellow-gold in the fall, with a blend of apricot and light red. This upright-growing tree gradually spreads at the top to make a fine-shaped specimen for landscaping. It attains a height of 26 ft. (8 m) or more and broadens to about 20 ft. (6 m). As an accent tree, it offers size, good form, interesting seasonal foliage changes, and outstanding bark color in the winter. It makes a striking color combination in the winter when planted near the contrasting green-barked cultivar 'Aoyagi'. The name means "coral tower," referring to the bark. Synonym, 'Senkaki'.

'Beni kawa' produces new growth that is bright salmon-red in the winter. The plant comes into leaf two weeks later than 'Sango kaku', has a slightly slower growth, and only reaches about 10 ft. (3 m) tall in 10 years.

'Fjellheim' arose from a witches' broom growing on 'Sango kaku' and has retained all the characteristics of its famous parent—the beautiful coral-red shoots and the five-lobed leaf shape, size, and coloring. The notable difference is that 'Fjellheim' is much bushier and shorter, forming a more compact bush.

'Saoshika'

Amoenum Group—green. The star-shaped bright green leaves are held out horizontally, giving a layered effect. New foliage is bright yellow-green with red or carmine lobe tips, becoming, in the summer, a uniform light green, darkening as summer advances. Fall color is a striking golden-yellow. The medium-sized, moderately deeply divided leaves have five to seven ovate lobes terminating in sharp points. The margins are lightly toothed. This plant makes a tall bushy shrub reaching 10 ft. (3 m) high and wide. Older twigs have a bright green bark. The name means "small male Japanese deer."

Acer palmatum 'Satsuki beni'. Photo by Francis Schroeder.

'Satsuki beni'

Amoenum Group—green. The medium-sized leaves are almost circular. The seven short lobes have narrow pointed tips and finely notched margins. Despite the name, which means "red month of May," this cultivar produces vigorous green leaves in the spring and summer. In the fall, the tree becomes brightly colored with flame and crimson foliage. 'Satsuki beni' forms a strong upright tree, reaching 26 ft. (8 m) in 20 years. It makes a good background tree in the landscape and can be used as a shade-producing cover tree for alpines.

'Sawa chidori'

Matsumurae Group—variegated. The medium-sized to large leaves have mainly seven deeply divided lobes with long tail-like tips and crinkled, coarsely toothed margins. The spring leaves emerge a light pink to blushed amber with a network of green veins, changing to whitish green with dark green veins for the summer. The shoots and leafstalks are a bright crimson. Fall color is a vivid red. This cultivar grows into a small to medium-sized bush. It needs some protection from hot sun and drying winds. The name means "marsh plover."

'Sazanami'

Matsumurae Group—green. The sharply pointed, rather small seven-lobed deeply divided leaves have a flat base and are distinctly and sharply toothed. The leaf shape gives a charming effect. Spring color is light orange-red, with the midveins a contrasting light green. Summer color is a rich green, and fall colors are strong gold blends. This slow-growing but hardy cultivar forms a large, compact bush, eventually reaching 16–20 ft. (5–6 m) tall and half as wide. The name means "ruffles."

'Seigai'

Palmatum Group—green. The brilliant scarlet spring foliage is the most attractive feature. The small moderately deeply divided leaves have five to seven lobes narrowing rapidly to sharp points. Margins are toothed. Spring color is bright crimson, lasting about a month, before the leaves

Acer palmatum 'Sawa chidori'. Photo by Cor van Gelderen.

Acer palmatum 'Sazanami'. Photo by J. D. Vertrees.

Acer palmatum 'Seigai'. Photo by Peter Gregory.

Acer palmatum 'Seigen'. Photo by Harry Olsen.

change to a bronze-green to blue-green and then the green of late summer, becoming flame-red in the fall. This hardy cultivar eventually makes a small upright tree or large shrub up to 13 ft. (4 m) tall. It is quite popular for bonsai. The name means "a blue cliff."

'Seigen'

Dwarf Group—green. The new leaves are bright fire-red, lasting for several weeks and similar to the popular 'Corallinum'. They become green for summer, turning yellow to persimmon in the fall.

This cultivar is one of the first to leaf and hence is susceptible to cold winds and spring frosts. The small five-lobed leaves appear dainty, are held close together, and are divided over halfway to the base. The margins are lightly toothed. 'Seigen' is similar to 'Tama hime' and 'Kiyohime'. It forms a small, rounded bush up to 6½ ft. (2 m) high. It is a favorite among the spring-colored dwarf cultivars and very popular for bonsai in Japan. The name means "clear dark color."

'Seiryū'

Dissectum Group—green. One of the few upright dissectums, this green laceleaf offers a pleasant contrast when planted with conventional dissectums. Each attractive bright green leaf is lightly tipped with reddish tones in the spring, changing to light green in the summer. In hot sun, the reddish tones may reappear on the margins. Fall colors are spectacular, ranging from strong gold to light yellows with a suffusion of crimson. The seven-lobed leaves are slightly smaller and not as finely cut as in most dissectums. The bark is a dark brown-green. The upright growth is quite strong with stiff, not willowy, new shoots. This desirable plant may reach 16–23 ft. (5–7 m) tall and 10–13 ft. (3–4 m) wide. The name means "blue-green dragon."

'Seiun kaku'

Palmatum Group—green. This upright flat-topped shrub, growing up to 10 ft. (3 m) tall, resembles a vigorous form of 'Mikawa yatsubusa'. Its small to medium-sized leaves are very similar, having long-ovate lobes with long, narrow, pointed tips. The central lobe is the longest. Margins are conspicuously coarsely toothed. As with 'Mikawa yatsubusa', the leaves overlap like the shingles on a roof. They are small and a deep green, turning a splendid red in the fall. The name may be translated as "palace in the blue cloud."

'Sekimori'

Dissectum Group—green. The leaf shape and color set this cultivar apart, as does the delightful green bark with a faint whitish dusting and distinct

Acer palmatum 'Seiryū'. Photo by Cor van Gelderen.

Acer palmatum 'Seiun kaku'. Photo by Peter Gregory.

white striations. Fall color is one of the best bright yellow-golds of the green dissectums. The medium-sized deep green leaves have five to seven lobes which are deeply but not finely cut to the midrib. The lobes look more feathery, while most green dissectums look lacier. 'Sekimori' is a strong, hardy plant, reaching 10–13 ft. (3–4 m) high and 13–16 ft. (4–5 m) wide. Planting it on a slope enhances its beauty. Oddly, the name means "a border guard post."

'Sekka yatsubusa'

Palmatum Group—green. This dwarf shrub differs from other dwarf plants in having leaves with narrower lobes. The small shiny, deep green leaves are deeply divided into five long-ovate

Acer palmatum 'Sekimori'. Photo by J. D. Vertrees.

Acer palmatum 'Sekka yatsubusa'. Photo by Harold Greer.

Acer palmatum 'Shaina'. Photo by Peter Gregory.

lobes with gradually tapering tips. The margins are very lightly toothed, and the tips of the tiny teeth turn up slightly, giving the edges a crinkled look. The red leafstalks are slender. New leaves are edged with a rust color. Fall color is yellow. The leaf nodes are close together, and the foliage is bunched. 'Sekka yatsubusa' reaches 10 ft. (3 m) tall. It is hardy and takes full sun well. The plant offers the choice of another small shrub for rock gardens, bonsai, and small plantings. The name means "dwarf that turns red," a reference to the spring color.

'Shaina'

Palmatum Group—red. This compact upright cultivar concentrates its round leaves in dense tufts on short shoots. Bright red in the spring, the leaves become dark purple-red in the summer and hold their color well until turning bright crimson in the fall. The five deeply divided lobes are narrowly long-ovate with pointed tips. Many of the center lobes are shortened with rounded tips—a char-acteristic of plants originating from witches' broom. 'Shaina' eventually forms a dense, globe-shaped shrub up to 10 ft. (3 m) or more and is ideal for container culture and rock gardens.

'Sharp's Pygmy'

Dwarf Group—green. The small green leaves of this outstanding dwarf turn deep orange to scar-let in the fall. The leaves are distinctly longer than wide. The five narrow deeply divided lobes are almost straplike, with tips tending to turn down. The center lobe is always much longer than the others, while the small basal lobes are held at a right angle to the leafstalk. The margins have coarse broad teeth. The short, slender leafstalks and shoots are green. 'Sharp's Pygmy' forms a densely foliaged, compact, low-spreading tree unlikely to reach 3 ft. (1 m) high. It needs no pruning or training to give it a bonsailike appear-ance, a truly remarkable dwarf.

'Akita yatsubusa' is similar in leaf and form to 'Sharp's Pygmy' but with dark brown shoots.

Acer palmatum 'Sharp's Pygmy'. Photo by Peter Gregory.

Acer palmatum 'Sherwood Flame'. Photo by J. D. Vertrees.

Acer palmatum 'Shigarami'. Photo by J. D. Vertrees.

'Sherwood Flame'

Matsumurae Group—red. The beautiful foliage is a rich reddish-purple approaching burgundy and holds its color better than most similar cultivars. The medium-sized seven-lobed leaves are divided almost to the base. The elongate-ovate lobes taper to very long, sharp points. The margins are deeply and regularly toothed. This vigorous, small tree makes a pleasant round-topped form and reaches 13–16 ft. (4–5 m) tall and up to 13 ft. (4 m) wide. It is an excellent specimen tree for the landscape, adding color in the spring and retaining the deep tones throughout the sum-

mer. 'Sherwood Flame' is almost identical to 'Burgundy Lace', but has slightly smaller leaves and the deep color does not fade in midsummer.

'Shidava Gold'

Dwarf Group—green. This highly desirable dwarf has bright yellow-green leaves contrasting with the pea-green bark. The five-lobed palmate leaves are moderately deeply divided. This cultivar is a miniature replica of its parent 'Aoyagi', with similar upright growth habit, leaf shape, toothed margins, and coloring through the seasons. It differs from its parent by having slightly smaller leaves and a shorter, more compact habit. 'Shidava Gold' is unlikely to reach 6½ ft. (2 m) tall under most conditions.

'Shigarami'

Amoenum Group—green. New foliage is bright green, with the light purple lobe tips becoming deeper purple in late spring. In the summer, the leaf becomes solid green. Fall colors are rich yellow and orange suffused with red. The medium-sized leaves have seven lobes which radiate stiffly outward, with the two very small basal lobes angled back along the leafstalk. Each moderately deeply divided lobe is long-ovate with almost parallel sides, then tapering gradually to a sharp tip. The lobe sides forming a slight trough. The margins have very fine teeth. The leaves are held stiffly horizontal by rigid leafstalks. This small upright tree has horizontal side branches giving it a layered appearance. It reaches a height of 13 ft. (4 m). The narrower, parallel-sided lobes and deeper leaf divisions of 'Shigarami' distinguish it from the similar 'Tana', which has broader triangular lobes and leaf divisions to halfway. The name means "posts in a river or stream to which boats are tied."

'Shigitatsu sawa'

Matsumurae Group—variegated. The leaf has a prominent green network of veins on a light yellow to yellow-green background. In the summer, the leaf darkens and the yellows become greener, while the network of veins becomes a darker

Acer palmatum 'Shidava Gold'. Photo by Peter Gregory.

Acer palmatum 'Shigitatsu sawa'. Photo by Peter Gregory.

Acer palmatum 'Shigure bato'. Photo by J. D. Vertrees.

Acer palmatum 'Shigure zome'. Photo by Peter Gregory.

green, sometimes with reddish main veins. In the fall, the leaves change to a unique red or rich red-green tone. The large leaves cup slightly upwards while the seven to nine broad ovate lobes radiate sharply outward, join about halfway to the base, and taper to long, sharp points. The margins have sharp regular teeth. This very old, fairly hardy plant appreciates some protection from the hottest sun. It is a medium-sized, upright grower, reaching 16 ft. (5 m) tall and up to 13 ft. (4 m) in spread. The name may mean "snipes quacking, flying up from a swamp" or it may refer to an ancient place name.

'Shigure bato'

Matsumurae Group—green. The beautiful small, seven-lobed, very deeply divided leaves have the tiny basal lobes angled backward, giving them a lovely feathery appearance. Each elongated lobe gradually tapers to a long tip which tends to curve down. The margins are deeply and irregularly toothed. The spring color is a brilliant red, turning green in the summer with the tips and edges remaining tinged red. Fall colors are gold to crimson. 'Shigure bato' forms an upright bush, attaining up to 10 ft. (3 m) high, and it may be as wide. It is tender. The name means "late fall rain."

'Shigure zome'

Amoenum Group—green. This very old Japanese cultivar has medium-sized leaves with seven moderately deeply divided lobes. Each lobe is ovate with a long tapering sharp tip and faintly toothed margins. In the spring, the leaves are purplish red and brownish red, becoming green in the summer with reddish leafstalks, and turning bright red to orange in the fall. 'Shigure zome' forms an upright tree up to 13 ft. (4 m) tall.

'Shikage ori nishiki'

Palmatum Group—red. Spring foliage is purple-red, changing to brownish red in the summer, gradually becoming greenish brown in late summer, and then turning orange in the fall. The large leaves are deeply divided into five to seven

Acer palmatum 'Shikage ori nishiki'. Photo by Cor van Gelderen.

long-ovate lobes with long slender tips and deeply toothed margins. The short stiff leafstalks are red. This cultivar is fairly hardy and forms a broad bush up to 13 ft. (4 m) tall.

Acer palmatum 'Shin chishio'. Photo by J. D. Vertrees.

Acer palmatum 'Shin deshōjō'. Photo by J. D. Vertrees.

'Shin chishio'

Palmatum Group—green. The extremely brilliant spring foliage turns a good green in the summer. The small leaves have five to seven moderately deeply divided ovate lobes tapering to well-defined tips. The margins are coarsely and sharply toothed. This multibranched, vigorous shrub grows up to 16 ft. (5 m) tall. It is among the best of the cultivars with bright pink-red spring color. It adapts well to container growing for patio display and for bonsai culture. It is known and sold mainly under the name 'Chishio Improved', which is illegitimate per the international cultivar code and should not be used. The name means "new Chishio," indicating its connection to a previously named cultivar.

'Shin deshōjō'

Palmatum Group—green. Spring leaves are a brilliant scarlet or crimson-scarlet which lasts a month or more before becoming a pleasant reddish green, then turning red and orange in the fall. The small leaves are moderately deeply divided into five to seven strongly ovate lobes with pointed tips. The margins have sharp teeth. The slender leafstalks and young shoots are red-brown to dark purple-red. This cultivar forms a shrub up to 10 ft. (3 m) high and 6½ ft. (2 m) wide. It is an excellent container plant for patio display and is popular as a bonsai plant. *Shin* means "new," implying that the plant is an improved selection of the well-known 'Deshōjō'.

'Shinobuga oka'

Linearilobum Group—green. The long, slender medium-sized leaves have five straplike lobes, which tend to hang down, giving a cascading appearance. The margins are smooth or lightly toothed. The bright dark green foliage holds its color well all season, changing to a pleasant yellow in the fall. This upright-growing plant grows to 10–16 ft. (3–5 m) tall. It is well adapted to container growing and provides interest in bonsai culture. Synonym, 'Linearilobum'.

'Shinonome'

Matsumurae Group—green. The spring foliage is bright orange-red, turning deeper red in the summer. Later, the leaves become green with a deep red overtone, accentuating the green midribs. The pink to orange-red second growth contrasts well with the bronze-green of late summer. The medium-sized leaves are deeply divided into seven elongate-ovate lobes with tips tapering to elongated, sharp points. The margins are markedly toothed. The slender leafstalks are deep red.

Acer palmatum 'Shinobuga oka'. Photo by Cor van Gelderen.

Acer palmatum 'Shinonome'. Photo by J. D. Vertrees.

Acer palmatum 'Shishi yatsubusa'. Photo by Cor van Gelderen.

Acer palmatum 'Shishigashira'. Photo by J. D. Vertrees.

'Shinonome' has an open growth habit and reaches up to 13 ft. (4 m) high. It offers a nice contrast when used in large plantings. Well-grown container plants make a fine display. The name means "eastern cloud in the early morning."

'Shishi yatsubusa'
Dwarf Group—green. The dense foliage is a good, strong green color which holds well all season and does not sunburn. Fall color is yellow. The leaves are divided into five lobes which are separated halfway to the flat leaf base. They are ovate with strongly pointed tips and very lightly toothed margins. This strong but stubby-growing dwarf shrub is popular for bonsai and of fairly easy culture. The name means "small lion cub."

'Shishigashira'
Palmatum Group—green. This cultivar is known for its bunched-up, heavily curled leaves at the end of short, stout shoots, which look like a lion's mane. The small leaf has five to seven deeply divided ovate lobes which taper to sharp points. The sides are curled upward, occasionally convoluted, and often forming a V-shaped trough, with mostly crinkled, coarsely but irregularly toothed margins. The leafstalks are short and stiff. The deep green foliage turns a stunning combination of gold suffused with rose and crimson tones in the fall. Usually a slow-growing plant, 'Shishigashira' can eventually reach 20 ft. (6 m) plus tall. The compact growth makes it very popular for small gardens, container culture, and bonsai. This unique cultivar always attracts attention. The name means "lion's head," referring to the shape of the leaf bunches which resemble Shishi, the mythical lion of Japanese drama.

'Shishio hime'
Dwarf Group—green. Leaf color is green with red edges and tips in the spring, becoming medium green for summer and changing to a bright yellow to gold in the fall. The small five-lobed leaves radiate outwards and are moderately deeply divided. Each lobe is ovate with a pointed tip and has deep evenly toothed margins. The long leafstalks are very slender. The growth habit is similar

Acer palmatum 'Shishio hime'. Photo by Harry Olsen.

Acer palmatum 'Shōjō'. Photo by J. D. Vertrees.

to that of 'Murasaki kiyohime' but smaller, forming a low, dwarf, dense, spreading shrub, reaching 3½ ft. (1.2 m) tall and wide. It is an excellent plant for container culture and bonsai.

'Shōjō'
Amoenum Group—red. The very deep purple-red almost black-red foliage holds its color well all summer. Fall color is crimson. The medium-sized leaves have five to seven deeply divided lobes which are elongate-ovate, terminating in slender points. The margins are regularly and lightly

Acer palmatum 'Shōjō nomura'. Photo by Harold Greer.

Acer palmatum 'Shōjō shidare'. Photo by Cor van Gelderen.

Acer palmatum 'Shōjō-no-mai'. Photo by Peter Gregory.

toothed. The slender leafstalks are red-brown. This cultivar becomes a wide, upright tree of at least 13 ft. (4 m) height. It is named after *Shōjō*, the red-faced monkey of Japanese dramas, and refers to the leaf color.

'Shōjō nomura'

Amoenum Group—red. The spring foliage is light red, changing to a distinctive bright red for summer, and turning scarlet in the fall. The medium-sized leaves have seven widely radiating lobes divided almost to the base. Each lobe is long-ovate tapering to a long sharp tip. The margins are finely toothed. The short leafstalks and shoots are red tinged with brown. 'Shōjō nomura' forms an upright rounded tree up to 16 ft. (5 m) tall. The name means "beautiful red-faced monkey."

'Shōjō shidare'

Dissectum Group—red. The spring leaves are maroon with the veins flushed dark green. The leaves become deep maroon in the summer, matching

the color of the short leafstalks and shoots. The medium-sized leaves are deeply divided into seven to nine lobes. The margins are irregularly toothed. This slightly tender cultivar forms a tall cascading dome up to 10 ft. (3 m) tall. The name means "cascading red-faced monkey."

'Shōjō-no-mai'

Palmatum Group—variegated. 'Shōjō-no-mai' is one of the best of the variegated palmatums with spring color. The basic leaf color is medium- to gray-green with attractive deep pink edging. The variegation causes the lobe tips to bend outward, creating a delightful windblown effect. The small irregularly shaped leaves are deeply divided into five long-ovate lobes which often have curved, sharply pointed tips. The margins are distinctly coarse-toothed. This cultivar is very similar to 'Beni shichihenge' in all aspects of growth, habit, and leaf, but differs from it in having a pure deeper pink leaf variegation in the spring. The name means "dancing red-faced monkey."

'Sister Ghost'

Matsumurae Group—variegated. Like other members of the Ghost series, this worthwhile Oregon selection has netted leaves. The medium-large leaves have seven deeply divided narrow curved lobes, with large sharply hooked teeth on the margins, and long tail-like tips. The leaves have a conspicuous network of green veins on a whitish-cream background, and look quite ghostly in a shady background. It is estimated this small bushy tree will eventually reach 13 ft. (4 m) tall. It needs some protection from the afternoon sun.

'Spring Delight'

Dissectum Group—green. A chance seedling with 'Viridis' as a possible parent, 'Spring Delight' is, as its name implies, very pretty in the spring. The emerging light green leaves are attractively edged in red which lasts into early summer. In all other respects, this cultivar is very similar to 'Viridis' in leaf appearance, vigor, and growth habit.

'Stella Rossa'

Dissectum Group—red. The very attractive pink-red spring foliage becomes a dark purple-red which lasts all summer before turning a bright red in the fall. The coloring is similar to that of 'Dissectum Nigrum', but the deep red is retained even longer. The large seven-lobed leaves are very deeply and finely dissected. The lobes themselves are deeply divided into relatively broad, flat sublobes with delicate fine saw-toothed margins. This vigorous pendulous dissectum from Italy forms a mushroom-shaped shrub up to 10 ft. (3 m) tall and 13 ft. (4 m) wide.

'Suisei'

Dissectum Group—variegated. This slow-growing Japanese dissectum is similar in leaf and variegation to the well-known 'Filigree'. Spring color is yellow-green. In the summer, the leaves are green with dense streaks of pale cream and specks of yellow on each side of the green

Acer palmatum 'Sister Ghost'. Photo by Peter Gregory.

Acer palmatum 'Spring Delight'. Photo by Harry Olsen.

Acer palmatum 'Stella Rossa'. Photo by Cor van Gelderen.

Acer palmatum 'Suisei'. Photo by Cor van Gelderen.

Acer palmatum 'Sumi nagashi'. Photo by Peter Gregory.

Acer palmatum 'Sunset'. Photo by J. D. Vertrees.

centers, this variegation gradually becoming pale green. Fall color is yellow to gold. The medium-sized deeply incised leaves have large sharply hooked and pointed teeth on the margins. 'Suisei' slowly forms a broad irregular mound up to 8 ft. (2.5 m) tall.

'Sumi nagashi'

Matsumurae Group—red. 'Sumi nagashi' is one of the best large-leaved red cultivars in its group. The deeply divided leaves have seven elongate-ovate lobes tapering gradually to thin, sharp points. The outer margins are double-toothed, the teeth with sharp, hooked tips. Spring color is bright purple-red, darkening to become almost black-red or very deep maroon. From midsummer, the color gradually changes to a deep green-red or brown-red. It greens up very readily in shade. Fall color is crimson. This vigorous, strong-growing, semiupright cultivar reaches 20 ft. (6 m) tall. It is an excellent tree for the garden landscape.

'Sunset'

Dissectum Group—green. This cultivar has non-typical dissectum leaf texture and color. The distinct lobes are dissected only once and range along both sides of the midribs, giving a sawtooth effect. Although they have a bright green base color, mature leaves have a distinctive overall tinting of rust, and leaves in full sun show a rusty to burnt orange tinting. The medium-sized leaves are held on fairly short leafstalks and are predominately yellow-colored in the spring. The cascading mounded habit is typical of most dissectums.

'Taiyo nishiki'

Palmatum Group—variegated. This sport from the popular 'Asahi zuru' differs from its parent in having yellow, not cream-white, variegation. The larger-than-normal leaves are deeply divided and mainly five-lobed. New leaves emerge with pink-flushed pale and deep yellow variegations on a

Acer palmatum 'Taiyo nishiki'. Photo by Peter Gregory.

Acer palmatum 'Takao'. Photo by Peter Gregory.

green background, becoming cream-colored to yellow on medium green for the summer. Fall colors are spectacular oranges and reds. This slow-growing cultivar eventually forms an attractive small tree. The name means "big-leaved brocade."

'Takao'

Palmatum Group—green. 'Takao' is an old cultivar with especially beautiful leaves. The medium-sized green leaves are divided into five to seven oblong-lanceolate lobes which taper to long, sharp tips. The margins are toothed. Fall color is bright yellow to gold. This cultivar forms a vigorous upright round-topped tree, growing up to 30 ft. (9 m) high at maturity. It is named after a place in Kyoto famous for its maples.

'Tama hime'

Dwarf Group—green. 'Tama hime' is a good dwarf for fall color. The tiny new leaves are a light green as they unfold, soon becoming a rich, shiny green, then turning red, crimson, and yellow in the fall. Each leaf has five ovate lobes which terminate in short tips and are moderately deeply

Acer palmatum 'Tama hime'. Photo by J. D. Vertrees.

separated. The margins are prominently toothed. The red leafstalks are quite short. This compact-growing, upright, vase-shaped, multibranched cultivar does not exceed 6½ ft. (2 m) high or wide. It is popular for bonsai. The name means "small globe."

Acer palmatum 'Tamuke yama' as an accent plant in the lawn. Photo by J. D. Vertrees.

'Tamuke yama'

Dissectum Group—red. The multidissected leaves have seven to nine lobes, which are not as deeply cut as in 'Crimson Queen' and 'Dissectum Nigrum'. Each lobe is broader and sturdier and ends in an extremely fine tip. New foliage is deep crimson-red, soon changing to a dark purple-red, an excellent color tone which holds well all summer. Fall color is a bright scarlet. The bark of the shoots and young branches is deep maroon, overcast with a whitish tone. This hardy plant is strongly cascading and grows to 13 ft. (4 m) tall. It is named after Mount Tamuke.

'Tana'

Amoenum Group—green. The beautiful foliage is light to yellowish green, with each lobe tipped in a distinct purplish-red that is similar to but not as deep as in 'Shigarami'. In the summer, the purple disappears leaving the leaves green. Fall color is a bright combination of gold and red. The lobes are separated halfway to the base and are broadly ovate, tapering to sharp points. The margins are very lightly toothed and curl slightly upwards. 'Tana' is a strong-growing, upright cultivar which reaches 20 ft. (6 m) tall. It becomes round-topped with a broad canopy. The name means "shelves," referring to the layered effect of the branches.

'Tatsuta'

Amoenum Group—green. Valued for the beauty of its scarlet fall color, this old cultivar is described by one Japanese reference thus: "The sun shines

Acer palmatum 'Tana'. Photo by Harry Olsen.   *Acer palmatum* 'Tatsuta'. Photo by Peter Gregory.

Acer palmatum 'Tennyo-no-hoshi'. Photo by Harold Greer.

on all the leaves and makes the fall foliage more beautiful." Spring leaves are a very light yellow-green soon changing to light green. The medium-sized leaves have seven lobes separated over halfway to the flat base. They are long-elliptic, with sharp tips and slightly toothed margins. 'Tatsuta' grows to a medium-sized shrub of up to 13 ft. (4 m) tall. It has open branches and a rounded top. It is named after a place in Japan.

'Tennyo-no-hoshi'

Palmatum Group—variegated. The chief attraction of this cultivar is the unusual, lightly variegated foliage. The small leaves have very narrow, deeply separated lobes. The margins are wavy and finely toothed. Base color is strong green with a cream or light creamy green variegation, mostly confined to a fine edging around each lobe. With the occasional stronger color break, the lobes develop a curve or twist. From a distance, the foliage has the appearance of a delicate cloud. Fall colors are a pleasant mixture of pale reds and rose. This cultivar is a strong grower and does well in full sun where the variegation has pink tones. It forms a medium-sized shrub of upright habit, eventually reaching about 13–16 ft. (4–5 m) high. The name means "angel's star."

'The Bishop'

Amoenum Group—red. The medium-sized purple-red leaves have seven deeply divided lobes. Each oblong-ovate lobe gradually tapers to a long, slender point. The margins are uniformly and finely toothed. The purple-red is bright in the spring and does not bronze until late summer. The fall color is an excellent crimson. This vigorous, upright-growing tree is hardy and reaches 13 ft. (4 m) at maturity.

'Tiger Rose'

Matsumurae Group—variegated. Originating in Oregon from a seedling of 'Azuma murasaki', this lovely variegated cultivar has the cascading shoots and semipendulous habit of 'Omure yama'. The deeply divided leaves have fingerlike lobes with crinkled edges. The new leaves emerge in the spring colored rose with pink tinges, becoming creamy white with green veins and margins for the summer. 'Tiger Rose' reaches 10 ft. (3 m) tall in 10 years and spreads 4 ft. (1.3 m) wide.

'Tobiosho'

Palmatum Group—green. This cultivar comes alive in the fall with its vivid scarlet color. The small leaves are deeply divided into five ovate lobes with tail-like tips. The margins are distinctly toothed. The red leafstalks are stiff and slender. 'Tobiosho' grows into an upright, wide-topped

Acer palmatum 'The Bishop'. Photo by Cor van Gelderen.

Acer palmatum 'Tiger Rose'. Photo by Peter Gregory.

Acer palmatum 'Tobiosho'. Photo by Harry Olsen.

Acer palmatum 'Toyama nishiki'. Photo by Cor van Gelderen.

Acer palmatum 'Trompenburg'. Photo by J. D. Vertrees.

medium-sized tree. It was named after the Oregon nurseryman who selected it.

'Toyama nishiki'

Dissectum Group—variegated. The basic leaf color is purple-red to greenish red. Some leaves lack variegation; others are completely pink as they first open in the spring. Most variegation shows up as pink or white portions on the lobes or blends into the leaf in endless variation. Because the leaves sunburn easily, plants grown in shade have more intense colors that hold better. The medium-sized leaves have seven to nine lobes, double-dissected, deeply cut to the midrib, and lacy. This tender, not very robust maple needs considerable care and attention. The name may be translated as "brocade of Toyama," a region in Japan.

'Trompenburg'

Matsumurae Group—red. This outstanding Dutch cultivar is popular wherever it is grown. The large unusual leaves have seven to nine deeply separated lobes, giving the appearance of fingers extended from a hand. Each lobe is oblong-ovate, with the edges rolled down, almost forming a tube. The margins are deeply toothed. The extraordinary leaf gives an unusual and pleasing effect to the whole tree. The stiff leafstalks are red, and the leaves are an outstanding rich purple-red color which lasts well into late summer. The foliage does not burn in full sun. Fall color is crimson. This upright grower reaches 20–26 ft. (6–8 m) high and 13–16 ft. (4–5 m) wide, and has become a favorite for landscaping. It is named after an arboretum in Rotterdam, Netherlands.

'Tsuchigumo'

Palmatum Group—green. 'Tsuchigumo' is a delightful semidwarf with small leaves. Spring leaves are rust-red, soon changing to bright green, this color holding well all summer. The leaves do not burn in full sun. Fall color is bright gold, with crimson edging. The interesting leaves have five to seven lobes separated almost to the base. Each lobe is elongate-ovate, tapering gradually to a sharp point. The margins of the lobes turn slightly

Acer palmatum 'Tsuchigumo'. Photo by J. D. Vertrees.

Acer palmatum 'Tsukomo'. Photo by J. D. Vertrees.

upwards and are conspicuously toothed. Some lobe tips curl downward. These leaves are similar to those of 'Shishigashira' but not as convoluted. This excellent small tree grows up to 13 ft. (4 m) tall. The name means "ground spider."

'Tsukomo'

Dwarf Group—green. This delightful dwarf bears spring leaves which unfold a bright, rusty red, becoming a light red-green, then a rich, deep green. The effect is quite beautiful as all the color phases appear together throughout the summer. Fall color is a strong yellow-gold. The leaves are deeply divided into five lobes which gradually taper to elongated tips. The margins are conspicuously double-toothed. The stiff leafstalks are green. This very choice and delightful dwarf is stubby and tends to grow upright. It makes a dense, dwarf mound reaching 3–5 ft. (1–1.5 m) high and wide.

'Tsukuba ne'

Palmatum Group—red. The medium-sized leaves are moderately divided into seven broadly ovate lobes which taper to long, slender points. The margins are evenly and delicately toothed. Spring color is light red with a green cast in the center, changing to a reddish green for the summer. The

Acer palmatum 'Tsukuba ne'. Photo by J. D. Vertrees.

green midveins are prominent. Fall color is a brilliant orange-crimson. This fairly vigorous, tall, upright-growing broad-topped tree grows up to 23 ft. (7 m) or so tall. It adds distinct colors to the garden landscape. The name means "ridge of Mount Tsukuba."

'Tsukushi gata'

Amoenum Group—red. This tree attracts attention in any garden and is one of the better dark-toned cultivars. The spectacular rich purple-red to black-red leaves hold their color well all season. The midveins of each lobe are a noticeable green contrast. The beautiful fruits are almost chartreuse-colored and seem to sparkle among the dark foliage. The large seven-lobed star-shaped leaves are divided to about halfway to the base. They are broadly ovate, tapering to sharp points. The leafstalks are light yellow-pink. This strong-growing plant forms a medium-sized round-topped spreading tree of 13 ft. (4 m) tall and almost as wide. It is named after a bay off Kyushu Island.

Acer palmatum 'Tsukushi gata'. Photo by J. D. Vertrees.

'Tsuma beni'

Amoenum Group—green. The outstanding feature is the purplish-red tips of the lobes in the spring. The upper margins of the lobes are the same color, the purple-red blending into the light green of the leaf center, becoming a shiny, darker green in the summer. Red colors dominate in the fall. The medium-sized five- to seven-lobed leaves are divided up to halfway to the base. Each lobe is ovate, terminating in a narrow tip. The margins are lightly and evenly toothed. This maple forms a rounded bush, reaching up to 10 ft. (3 m) tall and almost as wide. It is somewhat tender, but makes a very pleasant companion plant for dissectums and other shrubs. The name means "red nail," referring to the lobe tips in the spring.

'Tsuma gaki'

Amoenum Group—green. This cultivar resembles 'Tsuma beni'. As the leaves unfold, they tend to droop, adding a softness to the plant's general appearance. Spring color is a soft yellow-green. The lobe tips are shaded with persimmon-red to light purple-red blends. Summer color is deep green, and fall color is crimson. The medium-sized leaves have five ovate lobes tapering to slender tips and separated halfway to the base. The margins are evenly and lightly toothed. This maple forms a rounded plant up to 10 ft. (3 m) tall and wide.

'Tsuri nishiki'

Matsumurae Group—green. The interesting large seven-lobed leaves are widely separated and deeply divided. The narrow, almost lanceolate lobes terminate in long, tapering, sharp points and are sometimes twisted. The margins are roughly and sharply toothed. Spring color is a deep green with a tinge of red on the margins. In the summer, the leaves turn darker green. Fall colors are a brilliant yellow, orange-gold, and crimson. This cultivar is quite hardy and grows to a sturdy, medium-sized tree up to 16 ft. (5 m) tall.

'Ueno homare'

Palmatum Group—green. The small leaves are deeply divided into five lobes, each lobe elongate-ovate with a long slender tip. The margins are conspicuously toothed, giving the foliage a feathery appearance. One of the eye-catching maples with orange-yellow spring color, 'Ueno homare' is also one of the earliest to come into leaf. The spring leaves are deep yellow with orange-red edging, gradually changing to yellow-

Acer palmatum 'Tsuma gaki'. Photo by Cor van Gelderen.

Acer palmatum 'Tsuri nishiki'. Photo by J. D. Vertrees.

Acer palmatum 'Ueno homare'. Photo by Francis Schroeder.

green, then bright green in the summer, and turning a bright orange to red in the fall. This excellent, fairly vigorous small upright tree reaches 16 ft. (5 m) or so tall. It provides early spring color in the landscape. The name means "glorious Ueno," after a mountain in the Tokyo area with a park famous for its flowering cherries and flower-viewing parties.

'Ueno yama'

Palmatum Group—green. The outstanding spring-colored foliage is a deeper, brighter orange than that of 'Katsura'. The medium-sized leaves are deeply divided into five ovate lobes. The margins are coarsely toothed. 'Ueno yama' is one of the first cultivars to leaf out in the spring, and the intense orange color lasts for several weeks. Summer color is bright green. The fall colors are yellow to orange. In Japan, this medium-sized vigorous, upright-growing, hardy tree appears to be equated with 'Ueno homare." It is an excellent accent plant for medium-tall landscape needs and for early spring color. The name means "Mount Ueno."

'Ukigumo'

Palmatum Group—variegated. 'Ukigumo' is among the most outstanding variegated forms. Basic leaf color is light green, but most leaves are marked in varying degrees by white or pink spots, sometimes merging into large areas. Other leaves are totally white or light pink. The leaves are deeply divided into five lobes which radiate openly. Each lobe is long-ovate, ending in a sharp tip, and often twisted and wavy. The margins are finely and regularly toothed. This plant is not a rapid grower and needs some shade. It becomes a semidense shrub, reaching about 10 ft. (3 m) tall. The name means "floating clouds," referring to the soft pastel leaf colors blended in subtle combinations.

'Umegae'

Amoenum Group—red. The small leaves have seven ovate lobes separated halfway to the flat base and tapering to slender points. The margins are lightly toothed. The lobes fold slightly upward from the midribs. New foliage is bright brick-red, soon turning a bright purplish red. The green main

Acer palmatum 'Ueno yama'. Photo by Peter Gregory.

Acer palmatum 'Ukigumo'. Photo by Peter Gregory.

Acer palmatum 'Umegae'. Photo by J. D. Vertrees.

veins and yellow-green fruits make an attractive contrast. Fall colors are crimson tones. This slow-growing, upright yet spreading cultivar forms a round-topped bush that may reach 16 ft. (5 m) tall.

'Uncle Ghost'

Matsumurae Group—variegated. One of the Oregon Ghost series, this cultivar is similar in leaf shape and size to its parent, the well-known 'Beni shigitatsu sawa', but with a network of green veins on a paler whitish green background. It is especially noteworthy in the spring and early summer when the young leaves are pink-flushed from the outer margins. It is estimated to form a broad shrubby tree up to 10 ft. (3 m) tall and needs some protection from the afternoon sun.

'Utsu semi'

Amoenum Group—green. The margins of light green spring leaves are tinted purple or red. Later, the green becomes darker for the summer, turning crimson and purple in the fall. The large leaves have seven lobes divided halfway to the base. The broadly ovate lobes taper to short points and have finely toothed margins. This hardy cultivar forms a short, round-topped tree, reaching 13 ft. (4 m) tall and wide. It makes a fine landscape plant and adds contrasting spring leaf texture and excellent fall color. The name means "grasshopper skin," presumably referring to the shiny, bright green of the broad bold leaves.

'Vandermoss Red'

Matsumurae Group—red. The deep purple-red foliage is similar in color to that of 'Bloodgood', but the leaf lobes are narrower, more toothed, and more deeply divided and feathery. This cultivar holds its color very well, turning deep orange and vivid red in the fall. The large leaves are very deeply divided into seven long-ovate lobes, each with a long tail-like tip. The margins are distinctly and sharply toothed. The slender leafstalks are red. This vigorous plant forms an upright, wide, round-headed medium-sized tree up to 20 ft. (6 m) high.

Acer palmatum
'Uncle Ghost'. Photo
by Peter Gregory.

Acer palmatum
'Utsu semi'. Photo
by J. D. Vertrees.

Acer palmatum
'Vandermoss Red'.
Photo by Harold
Greer.

Acer palmatum 'Versicolor'. Photo by J. D. Vertrees.

'Versicolor'

Palmatum Group—variegated. This strong-grow-ing, hardy cultivar makes an upright broad-canopied tree exceeding 23 ft. (7 m) tall. Young bark is bright green, darkening with age. The leaves are deep green with white variegation, consisting of streaks, flecks, and patches. Where variegations are large, the lobes are sickle-shaped. Occasionally, pink colors are noticeable. The leaves have five to seven lobes and are at-tached to long, thin leafstalks. The lobes are ovate-acuminate with elongated tips. The mar-gins are shallowly double-toothed. The name means "variously colored."

'Villa Taranto'

Linearilobum Group—green. The starlike leaves of this excellent Italian strapleaf have five long, narrow, parallel-sided lobes. The center lobes are longest and create a lacy effect. The lobe margins are smooth. Emerging orange-crimson, the leaves soon become green with a light reddish overtone. The color is unique and is halfway between green and purple forms. In the fall, it turns a pleasing yellow to gold. This hardy cultivar forms a dome-shaped plant of 10 ft. (3 m) high. Its growth habit is very similar to that of 'Red Pygmy'. The name is after a famous Italian garden.

'Viridis'

Dissectum Group—green. Several green-leaved dissectums of good form are sold under this cultivar name. All of them have deeply dissected green foliage and form vigorous, strongly cascading shrubs of typical broadly mounded shape, eventually reaching up to 13 ft. (4 m) tall. The bright green summer color turns to gold, often tinged red, in the fall. The name means "green." Synonym, 'Viride'.

Acer palmatum 'Villa Taranto'. Photo by Harry Olsen.

Acer palmatum 'Viridis'. Photo by J. D. Vertrees.

Acer palmatum 'Wabito'. Photo by J. D. Vertrees.

'Wabito'

Palmatum Group—green. The small very unusual leaves have three to five lobes, each a slightly different shape. Separated almost to the base, the long narrow lobes are shallowly or deeply toothed. The teeth vary from blunt to sharp, flat or twisted, short or long. The pattern varies from one side of the lobe to the other, as well as between lobes and leaves. The total effect is a pleasing tattered appearance. Spring color is green with rose or rusty red margins, then green in the summer, changing to scarlet in the fall. This plant forms a small fastigiate shrub up to 10 ft. (3 m) tall. The name means "lonely person."

'Waka momiji'

Palmatum Group—variegated. The medium-sized leaves have five to seven deeply separated oblong lobes, each terminating in a long, slender tip. The margins are lightly toothed. Foliage is yellow-green with white variegation, which may consist of a few flecks to entire portions of the lobe but is often absent. In the spring, the variegation may be tinged with pink. The shoots are red in contrast to the green of 'Versicolor' and 'Oridono

Acer palmatum 'Waka momiji'. Photo by Cor van Gelderen.

nishiki'. This vigorous, upright, medium-sized tree forms a tall round-topped plant, probably reaching well over 23 ft. (7 m) tall.

'Wakehurst Pink'

Matsumurae Group—variegated. The large greenish leaves are flushed with pink in the spring, becoming greenish bronzed with pink dots and blotched variegation. A curious feature is that the outer lobes are very deeply divided, whereas the center lobe junction is about halfway to the flat base. The long-ovate lobes have tail-like pointed tips and regular sharply pointed hooked teeth on the margins. The leafstalks are purple-red. The upright growth habit is similar to that of 'Nicholsonii', forming an open-branched tree up to 13 ft. (4 m) tall and nearly as wide. This maple is named after Wakehurst Place Gardens, in Sussex, England, where the original plant was discovered.

'Waterfall'

Dissectum Group—green. The leaves are slightly larger than those of most dissectums, but otherwise typical. They are divided into seven to nine lobes, each lobe narrowly and deeply cut to the midrib. The distinguishing feature is that, because the lobes are held close together, they cascade and have a more flowing appearance. The foliage is a bright green and stands full sun well. Fall color is brilliant gold suffused with crimson. This cultivar is hardy and beautiful. The original plant in New Jersey was 10 ft. (3 m) high and 13 ft. (4 m) wide.

'Watnong'

Dissectum Group—red. The medium-sized leaves of this attractive New Jersey laceleaf have the coloring of the better-known red 'Baldsmith' and the finely cut lacy texture of the green 'Chantilly Lace'. New leaves are bright red, becoming salmon-pink before changing to pink-red over green for the summer. Fall colors are brilliant orange to scarlet. New red leaves are produced all summer and make an attractive contrast to the pink-green background of older leaves. The changing colors are more striking in full sun. 'Watnong' forms a

Acer palmatum 'Wakehurst Pink'. Photo by Harry Olsen.

Acer palmatum 'Waterfall'. Photo by J. D. Vertrees.

Acer palmatum 'Watnong'. Photo by Cor van Gelderen.

Acer palmatum 'Wendy'. Photo by Cor van Gelderen.

Acer palmatum 'Whitney Red'. Photo by Cor van Gelderen.

broad dense mushroom-shaped bush up to 10 ft. (3 m) tall and twice as wide.

'Wendy'

Palmatum Group—green. The attractive small, ivy-textured, semiglossy leaves have seven broadly ovate lobes with conspicuously large-toothed margins. New leaves are a delightful orange-pink, becoming bronze-red, and then changing to medium green, almost blue-green, with bronzed margins, thus producing a subtle multicolored effect throughout the summer. 'Wendy' forms a semidwarf spreading bush and is ideal for small gardens and containers.

'Whitney Red'

Amoenum Group—red. The vigorous tree with medium to deeply cut leaves is notable for its intense leaf color. The large five- to seven-lobed leaves emerge a deep purple-red with red venation, retaining their color well into late summer when they become a bronze-red. Fall color is vivid scarlet. The ovate lobes have tail-like tips and are deeply divided to the flat base. The margins are evenly toothed. The strong leafstalk is dark. 'Whitney Red' is vigorous growing with a habit similar to that of 'Bloodgood'. It becomes 20–26 ft. (6–8 m) tall and is named after Whitney Gardens in Brinnon, Washington, where the original plant was discovered.

'Wilson's Pink Dwarf'

Dwarf Group—green. The tiny leaves are divided into five slender lobes with toothed edges and are very colorful in the spring, when the entire plant is a light, bright pinkish or pink-red color. This brilliant spring coloring is quite noticeable in the landscape and lasts for several weeks. In the summer, the leaves become a bright, light green tone with pink to rusty red margins. This delightful, upright-growing dwarf shrub grows well and is vigorous. It was named after James Wilson, the California nurseryman who selected it.

'Coral Pink' is similar to 'Wilson's Pink Dwarf' and a much lighter, softer pink than 'Corallinum'. It merits a place in any garden landscape however small but prefers some shade.

Acer palmatum 'Wilson's Pink Dwarf'. Photo by Cor van Gelderen.

Acer palmatum 'Winter Flame'. Photo by Peter Gregory.

'Winter Flame'

Palmatum Group—green. This semidwarf, compact bushy form of 'Sango kaku' has bright coral-red winter shoots and more deeply divided leaves. The small to medium-sized leaves have seven lobes, the three middle lobes ovate-triangular with tail-like pointed tips. The small but distinct basal lobes are angled backward and outward. The slender leafstalks are red. Spring foliage is a lovely soft lime-green which contrasts beautifully with the pink-red shoots. Summer color is light green, turning attractive shades of yellow, orange, red, and light crimson in the fall. 'Winter Flame' reaches no more than 10 ft. (3 m) tall and is ideal for the small garden with colorful features year-round.

'Wou nishiki'

Matsumurae Group—green. The interesting medium-sized leaves are deeply divided into five to seven widely separated lobes. Each lobe is elongate-ovate and separated almost to the wedge-shaped base. The lobes taper to long, sharp tips. The margins are deeply toothed. The new leaves are a bright green, almost yellow-green, with margins strongly tinted with bright rose to rusty red. In the summer, the leaves become a light green. They take full sun well, only bronzing in extreme temperatures. Fall color is bright crimson. This upright-growing fastigiate plant reaches about 13 ft. (4 m) tall.

Acer palmatum 'Wou nishiki'. Photo by J. D. Vertrees.

Acer palmatum 'Yasemin'. Photo by Cor van Gelderen.

Acer palmatum 'Yezo nishiki'. Photo by Peter Gregory.

'Yasemin'

Matsumurae Group—red. This outstanding cultivar has large, deeply cut, shiny, attractive deep red foliage and red fruits. The leaves hold their color well into summer, becoming bronze-green. They are divided into seven to nine long-ovate lobes which spread widely, almost forming a circle. The tips are sharply pointed and the large margins are coarsely saw-toothed. The lobe edges have just a hint of being curved downward, but not as much as those of 'Trompenburg'. 'Yasemin' also differs from 'Trompenburg' by its darker leaf color and slightly flatter, wider lobes with larger teeth. 'Yasemin' is a vigorous upright-growing tree to 33 ft. (10 m) high. It was named by nurseryman D. M. van Gelderen for his granddaughter, Mirte Yasemin.

'Yezo nishiki'

Amoenum Group—red. The rich, bright reddish-purple spring color becomes deeper in the summer, then red-bronze. Fall tones are a stunning crimson and scarlet. The medium-sized seven-lobed leaves separate halfway to the flat base. Each lobe is ovate-acuminate tapering to a sharp point. The margins are evenly and finely toothed. The red leafstalks are slender. This upright, wide-spreading tree reaches 20–23 ft. (6–7 m) tall and spreads about 13 ft. (4 m). It is a hardy, sturdy selection.

'Yūbae'

Amoenum Group—variegated. This tall-growing cultivar has leaves with occasional variegation. The large leaves have deeply separated ovate

Acer palmatum 'Yūbae'. Photo by Cor van Gelderen.

Acer palmatum 'Yūgure'. Photo by J. D. Vertrees.

Acer palmatum 'Yuri hime'. Photo by Francis Schroeder.

lobes with tapering, pointed tips. The margins are slightly and irregularly toothed. The color is a strong, bold maroon to dark red, darkest in full sun. Variegation consists of patches and blobs of a lighter pink-red. The foliage is pleasant and attractive, even with no variegation present. This good dependable red cultivar forms a sturdy medium-sized tree reaching 16–20 ft. (5–6 m) tall. The name means "evening glow."

'Yūgure'

Matsumurae Group—red. The crimson spring foliage of this very old cultivar turns to rust-red with green hues in the summer, becoming red-crimson in the fall. The medium-sized leaves are moderately deeply separated into seven ovate lobes. Each lobe terminates in a sharp point and has lightly toothed margins. This hardy, upright round-topped tree reaches 16 ft. (5 m) or so tall and has very slender branches. The name means "twilight."

'Yuri hime'

Dwarf Group—green. The foliage lies closely over this small shrub, appearing as a covering of feathers. The small leaves have five very long, narrowly elongate-ovate lobes. The lobes are deeply separated and terminate in long, tapered points. The margins are finely toothed. The thin leafstalks are as long as the leaves. Leaf color is a strong light green, but the fall color is not outstanding. Although it is one of the smaller cultivars, 'Yuri hime' seems very hardy and takes full sun and exposure. It is a gem for miniature landscapes, such as alpine gardens.

OTHER *ACER* SPECIES
AND THEIR CULTIVARS FROM JAPAN

This chapter presents Japanese species and cultivars other than *Acer palmatum*. It also includes non-Japanese species and cultivars, such as *A. buergerianum* and *A. circinatum*, which have been selected and grown by Japanese horticulturists for their special characteristics.

Acer argutum
Pointed-leaf maple

This delightfully attractive species forms an upright small tree reaching 26–33 ft. (8–10 m) and makes an excellent companion plant. Lovely small green five-lobed leaves are remarkably uniform and divided about halfway to the base, prominently veined and covered in fine white hairs underneath. The broadly triangular-ovate lobes have pointed tips and sharp, even teeth on the margins. This species grows along moist streamsides and in mountain forests at elevations of 2640–6600 ft. (800–2000 m) above sea level, on the main Japanese islands of Honshu and Shikoku. The specific name means "sharp-toothed."

Acer buergerianum
Trident maple, three-pronged maple

This beautiful small upright Chinese species grows 33–42 ft. (10–13 m) tall. It is excellent for bonsai and container culture. Because of its tolerance to pollution and drought, it is widely used as a street tree in Japan and, as a result, has become naturalized there. The small leaves are three-lobed with rounded or angled bases. They are leathery with shiny mid to dark green upper surfaces and blue-gray to gray undersurfaces. When first emerging, the leaves are bronze-red and, in late fall, turn spectacular blends of orange, red, and purple. The name honors J. Buerger, who discovered the species.

Acer argutum. Photo by Peter Gregory.

Opposite: *Acer japonicum* 'Aconitifolium' (center) with *A. palmatum* 'Ornatum' (foreground). Photo by J. D. Vertrees.

Acer buergerianum.
Photo by J. D.
Vertrees.

Acer buergerianum
'Goshiki kaede'. Photo
by J. D. Vertrees.

'Goshiki kaede'. The basic color of the small leaves is a rich green with white variegation. The white ranges from completely covering the leaf to patches, streaks, or flecks. In the spring, the variegations emerge pink, turning to white, cream, and yellow. The name means "five-colored maple."

'Kōshi miyasami'. This vigorous dense shrubby tree up to 20 ft. (6 m) tall has small leaves with short bluntly pointed lobes. The spring leaves are a clear pink-red with yellow-green main veins, turning completely green in the summer and completely red in the fall.

'Kyūden'. This dwarf dense bush has small,

very thick, shiny, evergreen leaves. The lobes are short, rounded, and blunt-tipped. The new leaves are an attractive red-brown, becoming green for the summer, before turning yellow to orange in the fall. The name means "palace."

'Marubatō kaede'. The leaves are a bright shiny green, with a dominant long, bluntly tipped central lobe and short blunt side lobes in the outer third of the leaf. Fall color is a brilliant orange-red. This hardy cultivar forms an upright, round-topped small tree up to 30 ft. (9 m) tall.

'Mino yatsubusa'. The unusual, unmaple-like leaves are three-lobed and the long narrow central lobe has a sharply pointed tip and irregularly notched margins which tend to turn up to form a trough. The short stubby side lobes are near the base and radiate outwards from the leafstalk. The shiny rich green leaves turn brilliant scarlet and orange in the fall. This hardy cultivar forms a dense, rounded small shrub.

'Naruto'. The unusual leaves are divided into small long, narrow, sharply pointed lobes which are held like an upside-down T. The lobes have untoothed rolled margins to almost form tubes. The upper leaf surface is a deep rich green and the lower surface a soft gray-blue, so the rolled-up margins create a two-tone effect. Fall colors are a rich gold and red. 'Naruto' forms a tall dense sturdy plant up to 13 ft. (4 m) tall.

'Tanchō'. Resembling a dwarf form of 'Naruto', this very dense, round shrub has similar rolled-up two-toned leaves. Emerging a bronze-red in the spring, they become a rich green on the upper side during summer and turn orange blushed with red in the fall.

Acer capillipes
Hair-foot maple

This bold beautiful snakebark maple can become a large tree, usually maturing at about 39–50 ft. (12–15 m) high in cultivation. The attractive bark is green with light gray lengthwise stripes, becoming darker and slightly fissured with age. The three- to five-lobed medium-sized green leaves have a characteristic dominant broad triangular center lobe with a narrow, pointed tip and small

Acer capillipes. Photo by Peter Gregory.

shallow side lobes. Margins are irregularly toothed. The dominant center lobe, numerous hornbeamlike pairs of parallel lateral veins, and curious tiny light-colored bridges or pegs in the vein axils beneath make this maple easily recognizable. The leafstalks and young shoots are an attractive pink-red to scarlet from the time they appear in the spring and throughout the growing season. Fall produces a galaxy of colors from yellow to scarlet, often all colors occurring on the tree at the same time. While this tree is native throughout Japan, it is concentrated only in the mountain areas around Tokyo. The specific name means "hairlike."

Acer carpinifolium
Hornbeam maple

The characteristic medium-sized green leaves of this very atypical maple are distinct and closely resemble those of *Carpinus*, the hornbeam. They have the same rough-textured surfaces, long ovate-oblong shape, tail-like tip, numerous

Acer carpinifolium. Photo by J. D. Vertrees.

Acer caudatum subsp. *ukurunduense.* Photo by Peter Gregory.

conspicuous parallel lateral veins, and coarse, sharply toothed margins. This large multistemmed shrub or small tree matures at 26–39 ft. (8–12 m), forming a wide-spreading mushroom-domed crown. It is hardy and durable, and makes an outstanding specimen plant for landscaping. Native to Japan, it is common in temperate deciduous forests on moist soils at elevations of 660–4290 ft. (200–1300 m) above sea level. The specific name means "leaves like *Carpinus*."

Acer caudatum subsp. *ukurunduense*

This variable-growing plant forms a large shrub or small tree 23–33 ft. (7–10 m) tall. It is often multistemmed. The light gray-brown bark of older trunks peels off in small, thin flakes. The young shoots are reddish and covered with short hairs, soon becoming yellow-brown. The medium-sized leaves are whitish green above, with a dull yellowish pubescence underneath. The five lobes are ovate-triangular with short-pointed tips. The margins are sharply and coarsely toothed. While the species is native to the Himalayas, northern India, and western China, the subspecies *ukurunduense* is more widely distributed in Japan, the Kurile Islands, Korea, southeastern Siberia, and Manchuria.

Acer circinatum
Vine maple

Although it is not native to Japan, *Acer circinatum* is a close relative of the Japanese *A. palmatum* and *A. japonicum*, and is able to hybridize

Acer circinatum 'Little Gem'. Photo by Peter Gregory.

Acer cissifolium. Photo by Peter Gregory.

with them. It is native to the Pacific Northwest and can form a small tree up to 26 ft. (8 m) tall or, more often, a wide-spreading multistemmed shrub, with snaky vinelike slender stems. It is most appreciated for its beautiful fall colors—a brilliant scarlet suffused with orange and yellow tones. In the spring, the medium-sized round leaves are a bright green. They have seven to nine shallow lobes, with distinctly but shallowly toothed margins. This maple is an excellent trouble-free small tree for the garden landscape where it is a good companion for many types of perennials and shrubs. It is perfectly hardy and tolerates most conditions of soil, sun or shade, drought or moisture.

'Little Gem'. This beautiful dwarf has a tiny round leaf with seven to nine ovate-triangular lobes with lightly toothed margins. The foliage is a light green color with a very lightly wrinkled surface. Fall colors are orange and crimson. This cultivar forms a compact, rounded shrub up to about 3 ft. (1 m) tall and wide.

'Monroe'. Unlike most cultivars of *Acer circinatum* which have shallowly lobed leaves, 'Monroe' has dissected leaves. The five to seven lobes are separated entirely to the base, with the sides of each lobe deeply cut, almost to the midrib. These sublobes are toothed, forming very irregular margins. This sturdy plant forms an upright bush to 13 ft. (4 m) tall, becoming broad with age.

'Sunglow'. This distinctive, small cultivar has very small, circular leaves, which are pretty, especially in the spring when they emerge a peach to light orange-apricot color. This color lasts for four to six weeks, becoming a medium green for the summer. In the fall, the color turns to plum red, purple, and crimson. The seven-lobed leaves are shallowly divided. Each lobe is broadly ovate with short pointed tips and irregularly toothed margins. Slow-growing, this bushy plant forms a small round ball and reaches a little over 3 ft. (1 m) in 10 years. Like many other dwarf cultivars, it is susceptible to mildew attacks. It is very different from any other *Acer circinatum* cultivar and highly desirable.

Acer cissifolium
Vine-leaf maple

Composed of three leaflets, the leaves are similar in shape to some of the *Cissus* (grape ivy) species, hence the species and common names. The young leaves emerge a light yellow-green, often pink-tinged to bronzed, before becoming a light to medium green for the summer. In the fall, they turn yellow with pink tones, finally becoming a fiery red. The leaflets are fairly uniform in shape and size. Each one is ovate with a tail-like tip, wedge-shaped base, and coarsely toothed margins. The long, slender leafstalk is bright red and has a broad, swollen base which completely encloses the bud. Native to Japan, this species grows in moist conditions in the lower montane forests at elevations of 660–4290 ft. (200–1300 m) above sea level. It is perfectly hardy, relatively easy to grow, and enjoys moist situations in cultivation. It forms a small to medium-sized tree with a wide-spreading mushroom-shaped crown, reaching 33–50 ft. (10–15 m) tall and about as wide.

Acer crataegifolium
Hawthorn maple

An excellent small tree for landscaping and as a companion plant for flowering shrubs and perennials, *Acer crataegifolium* does not become too large, usually up to 26 ft. (8 m) tall. It is hardy, holds its foliage color very well, and stands full sun. The small three-lobed leaves have a distinct shape—long, triangular-ovate with a tapering tip and a heart-shaped to rounded base. The two very small side lobes are occasionally absent, and the margins are irregularly serrated and slightly wavy. Leaf color is a pleasing blue-green above, often bronze-purple with purplish margins, shiny and purplish green beneath. One of the smallest snakebark maples, this species has green bark with indistinct faint white to dark gray striations. Young shoots are purple-red to green. The species grows wild in the central and southern regions of Japan, preferring dry, sunny situations. The specific name means "leaves like *Crataegus*," referring to the hawthorn genus.

'Veitchii'. The leaves of this selection are the usual shape and size for the species—triangular-ovate, tapering to a slender tip—but with spectacular variegations. The base color is blue-green. The white to cream and gray-green markings appear on the leaf as specks, flecks, or "cut-in" sections, or sometimes completely covering the leaf. Pink flecks or streaks are often intermixed with the white. Some leaves are entirely white, while others have no variegation. In the fall, the white portions become rose-pink to scarlet. This cultivar forms a tall dense shrub or small tree, reaching 20 ft. (6 m) high. It is named after a famous British nursery which introduced many plants into cultivation.

Acer crataegifolium 'Veitchii'. Photo by J. D. Vertrees.

Acer diabolicum. Photo by Peter Gregory.

Acer diabolicum
Devil maple, horned maple

This species is distinguished by curious hornlike stigmas which persist at the inner junction of the fruit nutlets, resembling the horns of the devil. The large, five-lobed, thick-textured leaves are up to 6 in. (15 cm) long. The lobes are divided to about halfway to the leaf base. The middle three lobes are broadly lanceolate-ovate, with short acuminate tips. The two basal lobes are short and small. The margins are irregularly, coarsely, and bluntly toothed. Leaf color is medium to deep green. This strong, medium-sized, sturdy tree reaches 33–50 ft. (10–15 m) tall with a fairly broad, rounded canopy. It can be one of the most spectacular maples in flower, particularly when the bunches of large red male flowers appear. A flowering tree has been described as "looking like the smoldering embers of a gigantic bonfire." This maple is native to Japan, common in the north, less frequent in the south. It is found in open areas on sunny lower mountain slopes from 1320 to 4290 ft. (400–1300 m) above sea level.

Acer distylum. Photo by Peter Gregory.

Acer distylum
Lime-leaved maple

This rare Japanese species has very distinctive un-lobed heart-shaped leaves, hence its common name. It occurs in the mountains of north and central Honshu and grows on moist soils at 2275–5200 ft. (700–1600 m) above sea level. The spring leaves are an attractive light gray dusted a sandy or pinkish hue, becoming medium to dark green for summer, and turning a clear bright yellow in the fall. *Acer distylum* becomes a medium-sized tree up to 33–49 ft. (10–15 m) tall and would make a very attractive landscape plant.

Acer japonicum
Fullmoon maple

An important feature of this species is the brilliant fall colorings—yellow, orange, and red—making this maple worthwhile for landscaping. Most forms of the species are sturdy, strong-growing trees, adaptable to most garden situations. The large rich green leaves are round and usually have 9–11 lobes. Each lobe is shallowly separated and tapers rapidly to a point. Margins are lightly to coarsely toothed. *Acer japonicum* is a desirable, small to medium-sized tree reaching 33 ft. (10 m) high. It is native to Japan.

'Aconitifolium'. Fern-leaf maple. This popular and bold cultivar has large leaves with 9–13 deeply cut lobes which divide almost to the leaf base. Each lobe is again deeply divided, the sublobes irregularly dissected, producing a fern-like appearance. The leaf form approaches that of the monkshood genus, *Aconitum*. The inner one-third of each lobe narrows almost to the midrib, giving an open form to the center of the leaf. The foliage is deep green, with tufts of hairs at the vein junctions beneath. Fall colors are brilliant scarlet shaded with carmine and sometimes purple. Clusters of maroon winged fruit add to the attractiveness. This strong plant forms a round-topped small tree, reaching a height of 16 ft. (5 m). It is one of the largest-leaved forms of the fullmoon maple and one of the most desirable for any size landscape.

Acer japonicum 'Aconitifolium'. Photo by J. D. Vertrees.

Synonym, 'Maiku jaku' (meaning "dancing peacock").

'**Green Cascade**'. This unique selection is a weeping form, almost prostrate. It is best grown on a bank where it can cascade down to form a green mantle. Young plants should be staked to form a center stem from which the limbs can cascade. Each medium-sized leaf is a rich green with 9–11 lobes separated to the leaf base. The lower end of each lobe is very little wider than the midrib, then the lobe becomes broad but is deeply dissected to give the leaf a lacelike effect. Fall colors are a brilliant yellow-orange and crimson.

'**Ō isami**'. The lobes of the large round leaves are separated about halfway to the leaf base. The tapering ends of the lobes are deeply notched. New leaves are light yellow-green, becoming a rich green which persists well into the fall without sun burning. Fall colors are red and yellow blends. This vigorous plant forms a round-topped, medium-sized tree which reaches 23–26 ft. (7–8 m) or more tall.

'**Ō taki**'. The leaves have 9–13 lobes which are divided about halfway to the leaf base. Margins are deeply toothed, giving a feather-edge appearance. The leaf surface is sometimes sparingly covered with fine, silvery hairs. Spring and summer colors are a deep, rich green, almost a blue-green in partial shade. Fall color is outstanding with red, crimson, gold, and orange blends. This maple forms a small tree up to 13 ft. (4 m) tall. The name means "big waterfall."

'**Vitifolium**'. The large leaves resemble those of the grape genus, *Vitis*. They are deep green with 9–11 lobes. Each lobe is separated almost halfway to the leaf base and terminates in a sharp point. The main veins show distinctly as a lighter green. Fall colors are magnificent: the golds, tinged with crimson and scarlet at first, change to a vivid scarlet. This strong-growing, upright tree becomes broad and round-topped, reaching at least 33 ft. (10 m) tall and wide.

Acer maximowiczianum
Nikko maple

This sturdy, medium-sized to large tree has a broad, round crown and matures at 46–66 ft. (14–20 m) high. Its most distinctive feature is the

Acer maximowiczianum.
Photo by Peter Gregory.

stout, dense hairiness of all its parts—shoots, leaves, leafstalks, flower stalks, and fruits. The medium-sized leaves have three relatively large, almost stalkless, ovate, irregularly bluntly toothed or wavy edged leaflets with bluntly pointed tips. The upper surface is a matt medium to dark green, with an attractive blue-gray to gray underside thickly felted with stiff gray hairs. This maple is among the last to change color in the fall, beginning with subtle pastel shades of yellow and pink, turning to orange and red, and becoming a deep flaming red which lasts well into late autumn. Native to Japan, this species extends into China, growing in the lower montane forests on moist well-drained fertile valley soils at elevations of 1650–5940 ft. (500–1800 m) above sea level. The specific name honors Russian botanist Carl Maximowicz. Synonym, *Acer nikoense*.

and adaptable. The foliage and shoots are an enchanting bright red when they first appear in the spring and contrast well with the numerous greenish-white flowers. The dainty, small, five-lobed leaves with tail-like tips change to green. They pass through various shades of orange, pink, and scarlet in the fall to become a fiery red. The lobes are long-ovate with long slender tips and strongly toothed margins. The dominant center lobe is the largest. The tiny flowers appear as festoons hanging through the foliage and develop into chains of small attractive red-tinged fruits. This species forms a tall shrub or small tree up to 37 ft. (11 m) high. Native to Japan, it grows in open, sunny areas of the forests of the middle and upper mountain slopes at elevations of 2310–7590 ft. (700–2300 m). The specific name means "small-flowered."

Acer micranthum
Small-flowered maple

Acer micranthum is another of the delicate-appearing species of snakebark maples and one of the smallest. It is not fragile, however, but hardy

Acer miyabei
Miyabe's maple

This medium-sized to large sturdy tree reaches 50–82 ft. (15–25 m) tall and forms a broad canopy. The five-lobed leaves are similar to, but

Acer micranthum. Photo by Peter Gregory.

Acer miyabei. Photo by Peter Gregory.

larger than, those of the European field maple, *Acer campestre*, to which it is closely related. The lobes separate to about halfway, are rectangular-ovate with acuminate, bluntly pointed or rounded tips, and irregularly lobulate teeth. The leafstalks contain a milky sap. Young leaves are covered with short hairs on both sides and become a matt olive-green in the summer. The fall color is a buttercup-yellow. Native to Japan, *Acer miyabei* grows in moist woods along streamsides throughout northern and central Honshu. The specific name honors Japanese botanist Kingo Miyabe.

Acer morifolium
Yaku maple

This small snakebark maple grows 39–49 ft. (12–15 m) tall and is closely related to the hairfoot maple, *Acer capillipes*. The medium-sized leaves have three to five ovate-triangular lobes with tail-like tips, strongly toothed margins, and a dominant central lobe. The new leaves are an attractive shiny bronze-green, becoming mid to

dark green with a slight sheen for the summer, before turning yellow to gold flushed with red in the fall. The specific name means "leaves like *Morus*," the mulberry genus.

Acer pictum
Painted maple

This hardy, very variable species, also known under the name *Acer mono*, is a fast-growing medium-sized to large tree which develops a rounded, spreading canopy, and reaches 33–46 ft. (10–14 m) high. It is a fine selection for overstory shade in perennial and shrubbery plantings. The painted maple has a wide distribution from central and northeastern China and Manchuria, eastern Siberia, Korea, and throughout Japan. The five- to seven-lobed medium-sized leaves are usually shallowly divided one-quarter to one-third of the way to the base. The lobes are short, broad, and triangular-ovate, with tail-like sharply pointed tips. The margins are untoothed. The long green leafstalks contain a milky sap. The leaves are bright to matt green throughout the

Acer morifolium, fall color.
Photo by Douglas Justice.

Acer pictum 'Hoshi yadori'.
Photo by J. D. Vertrees.

Acer pictum 'Usugumo'.
Photo by J. D. Vertrees.

spring and summer, turning brilliant gold tinged with crimson in the fall.

'Hoshi yadori'. The remarkable foliage has both starlike specks and sand-dusted white to cream variegations boldly covering the deep green base color in varying amounts from light dots to bold color slashes. In full shade, the markings are almost pure white. In sun, they are a light yellow to gold. Full exposure to hot sun, however, causes leaf damage. The leaves have five to seven broadly triangular shallow lobes This cultivar forms a compact medium-sized shrub up to 16 ft. (5 m) tall. When it is sited near a path, the unique foliage can be easily seen and appreciated. The name means "star leaf."

'Usugumo'. This most unusual leaf form has been likened to a bat's wing. However, the large seven- to nine-lobed leaf is more beautiful than this term would indicate. The "fabric" appears to be stretched between the sharp-pointed end and the prominent main vein in each lobe. Each lobe is broadly triangular and terminates in a sharp point. The green leaves are thickly speckled with very fine white dots, making the leaf appear whitish green. A narrow, almost pure white strip runs along each side of the strong green main vein of each lobe. Spring leaves are an unusually pale pink-yellow before becoming whitish green for summer. This upright slow-growing maple reaches 10–13 ft. (3–4 m) high.

Acer pycnanthum
Japanese red maple

Native to Japan, this species grows on the lower mountain slopes in moist swampy ground and is closely related to the North American red or swamp maple, *Acer rubrum*. The irregularly shaped leaves are rounded to triangular, usually with three shallow indistinct lobes, and irregular, bluntly toothed margins. The upper surface of new leaves is attractively bronzed to deep red, becoming green for the summer, and with lovely blue-gray undersides which catch the eye as the leaves flutter in the breeze. *Acer pycnanthum* can reach more than 80 ft. (24.5 m) tall and is useful as an overstory tree in mixed landscapes. The specific name means "flowers in dense clusters."

Acer pycnanthum. Photo by Peter Gregory.

Acer rufinerve 'Winter Gold'. Photo by Robert Jamgochian.

Acer rufinerve
Red-veined maple
This strong-growing, upright tree reaches 39–50 ft. (12–15 m) tall. It is one of the attractive snakebark maples with dark, narrow, lengthwise gray stripes running up the lustrous green surface. With age, the stripes become grayer. The most unusual character of the species is the soft bluish-gray bloom covering the new shoots. The medium-sized leaves are five-lobed, with the pair of tiny basal lobes and the middle three lobes pointing forward. The dominant center lobe is triangular. The margins are toothed. The upper surface is medium to dark green, the undersurface a lighter green with dense rusty-brown hairs along the veins. These reduce to tufts in the vein axils later in the season. Fall colors are rich yellow and gold suffused with crimson. In Japan, this species grows in the middle and upper parts of the mountain forest slopes, up to an elevation of 6600 ft. (2000 m). It adapts well in gardens, accepting dry and moist situations, although it prefers sunny, moist conditions. The specific name means "red-brown."

Acer rufinerve. Photo by J. D. Vertrees.

'Albolimbatum'. Leaf size and shape are typical of the species, but the amount of white and gray-green variegation in its deep green foliage varies greatly. The edges are usually tinged with white, sometimes as a very thin band, but on some leaves the markings are scattered in specks, splashes, and patches and extend over the whole leaf. Some leaves are entirely free of any variegation. This slow-growing, upright tree is smaller than the species, attaining 33–39 ft. (10–12 m) tall. Synonym, 'Hatsu yuki'.

'Winter Gold'. This notable addition to the larger trees has interesting shoots. In the summer, they are yellow-green. The winter color is a bright golden-yellow which readily attracts attention. The foliage is typical for the species, but the fully grown tree is slightly smaller. This cultivar is quite striking when planted near the red-barked Acer palmatum 'Sango kaku'.

Acer shirasawanum
Shirasawa's maple
The total effect of the foliage texture and color makes this species a desirable choice as a companion tree for shrubbery plantings. Leaf texture is unlike that of related species in having the feeling of stiff, thin, almost translucent paper. Though appearing delicate, the leaves resist sunburn more than those of most maples. The light yellow-green young leaves are covered in soft white hairs, becoming smooth, hairless, and a

Acer shirasawanum 'Aureum'. Photo by J. D. Vertrees.

light tone of lime-green. Fall color is gold with crimson blends. The small round leaves have 9–13 short ovate lobes which separate only a third of the way to the base. The leaves are saucer-shaped because of the slight "pleating" along the numerous main veins. The ovate lobes terminate in short, pointed tips and have prominently toothed margins. The new shoots are bright green and sometimes have a gray bloom. Growth is slender and mature trees rarely exceed 33 ft. (10 m) in cultivation. This species is native to central and southern Japan, where it grows on moist well-drained mountain valley slopes at elevations ranging from 2310 to 5940 ft. (700–1800 m) above sea level. The specific name honors Japanese botanist Homi Shirasawa.

'**Aureum**'. Golden fullmoon maple. This yellow-leaved form is highly prized. The spring foliage is bright yellow, becoming yellow-green to medium green in the summer. This cultivar tolerates full sun better than most yellow forms, but in partial shade, the foliage retains the yellow tones a little longer than in the bright sun. The fall colors are often spectacular, varying from orange through red and occasionally with purple blends. The smallish leaves are typical in size and shape for the species. This lovely small tree has bright red fruits in light bunches projecting up through the golden foliage, adding another attractive feature to this fine plant.

'**Autumn Moon**'. This small tree has attractive foliage of an unusual burnt-orange color with an underlying shade of base green. These colors are strongest when the plant is in full sun. Shaded leaves carry pale yellow-green tones. In the fall, the leaves turn rich orange and red. The smallish leaves are in the shape typical of the species. The prominent midribs are a rusty color on some leaves. This cultivar seems to stand heat well and is best grown where plenty of sunlight develops the colors.

'**Microphyllum**'. The small rounded leaves are slightly cupped at the attachment to the leafstalk. The basal lobes overlap and, with the

Acer shirasawanum 'Microphyllum'. Photo by Ray Prag.

upturn of the leaf, form a shallow cup. The red leafstalks are sturdy. Leaf color is dark green, becoming bright blends of reds and yellows in the fall. The growth seems less vigorous than that of the species, but the plant forms a small tree to 20 ft. (6 m) tall. It appears to be a sturdy and hardy form. The name means "small-leaved."

'Ogura yama'. The brilliant display of rich orange and scarlet blends in the fall makes this a favorite medium-sized maple. Spring foliage is a light yellow-green, changing to green with a silvery overcast due to a covering of extremely fine hairs. The hairs disappear in midsummer. 'Ogura yama' is similar to 'Microphyllum' in appearance and leaf but is slower growing, reaching about 13 ft. (4 m) tall. It makes a sturdy, hardy plant. The name means "Mount Ogura."

'Palmatifolium'. This very beautiful selection has distinct foliage which is very attractive in all seasons. The bright green leaves take full sun without burning. The fall colors are very spectacular and persist for a long period, blends of yellow and gold, mottled and shaded crimson. The medium-sized leaf has 11 lobes which are long, ovate-acuminate with sharp, narrow tips, separated distinctly over halfway to the leaf base. The margins roll slightly downward, making the separation between lobes more distinct. Shoots are a dusty green with prominent white striations. This sturdy, upright small tree forms a rounded canopy and matures at about 26 ft. (8 m) high. It is hardy and accepts a wide range of culture conditions. The name means "palmate-leaved."

Acer sieboldianum
Siebold's maple

The bright green small to medium-sized leaves are round with 7–11 ovate lobes separating up to halfway to the base. Each lobe terminates in a sharp point and has sharply toothed margins. The undersurface and leafstalks are covered with a fine white down at first, which diminishes during the summer. Fall color is outstanding, turning a brilliant scarlet with some orange. This species is one of the most common in the mountain woods and thickets of Japan. It forms a tall multistemmed shrub or small tree up to 33 ft. (10

m) tall. It can be depended upon for fall color and makes a very hardy, trouble-free plant for mixed landscapes. The specific name honors German botanist Philipp F. von Siebold.

'Kinugasa yama'. The foliage is a distinct blue-green color and heavily covered with silvery hairs. Fall colors are blends of brilliant orange and red. The medium-sized leaves have seven to nine lobes which separate at least halfway to the base. 'Kinugasa yama' is a stocky, round-topped small tree which reaches 20–23 ft. (6–7 m) high. The name means "silk umbrella," referring to the silky hairiness of the leaves.

'Sode-no-uchi'. This dwarf cultivar has the smallest leaves of any form of the species. The foliage is a bright, light green which holds well through the summer. Fall colors are mainly bright yellow with red tones. The seven to nine lobes radiate evenly outward and are separated at least halfway to the leaf base. This attractive little plant tends to form a rounded bush, making it popular for bonsai in Japan as it requires little pruning. It fits well into many types of planting, particularly in alpine gardens and in containers on patios.

Acer tataricum subsp. ginnala
Amur maple

The Amur maple is one of the hardiest small maples. It forms a multistemmed, dome-shaped large bush or small tree, reaching 26 ft. (8 m) or so high. The tree is quite trouble-free and adapts to most cultural conditions. The three-lobed small to medium-sized leaves have an oblong-triangular center lobe which is much more prominent and longer than the two short side lobes. The lobe tips are pointed, and the margins are coarsely toothed. The foliage is bright green all season, durable, and withstands full sun. Fall color is a spectacular display of bright scarlet. A bonus is the copious production of bunches of bright red fruits beginning in early summer. The Amur maple grows wild in northeastern China, Manchuria, North Korea, and the islands of Japan. The subspecific name *ginnala* is also a local name for this maple.

'Bailey Compact'. This dwarf cultivar has a dense compact habit. The leaf shape is typical for

Acer sieboldianum 'Kinugasa yama'. Photo by J. D. Vertrees.

Acer sieboldianum 'Sode-no-uchi', spring color. Photo by J. D. Vertrees.

Acer tataricum subsp. *ginnala*. Photo by Peter Gregory.

the subspecies but slightly smaller. The foliage turns a bright shiny red in the fall. 'Bailey Compact' is ideally suited for the small garden or as a container plant.

'Embers'. This fast-growing broad tree reaches 19 ft. (6 m) tall and spreads 13 ft. (4 m) across. It has clusters of red fruit protruding from the glossy green leaves, and an eye-catching red fall color. 'Embers' makes a fine specimen or patio tree.

'Emerald Elf'. Rarely exceeding 6 ft. (1.8 m) tall and wide, this compact dense rounded dwarf has glossy green foliage which turns a vivid burgundy-red in the fall. 'Emerald Elf' prefers full sun or light shade and makes an excellent patio or container plant.

'Flame'. This medium-sized shrubby tree to 23 ft. (7 m) tall has stunning fall color. The leaves are a typical shape and size for the subspecies. Colored a glossy green, they contrast with clusters of red fruits from early summer onwards. Fall color is a fiery red. 'Flame' makes a fine specimen tree. It can also be used in a shrub border.

Acer truncatum
Purple-blow maple

This species is very closely related to and quite similar to the painted maple, *Acer pictum*. Native to northern China, Manchuria, Siberia, North Korea, and the Japanese island of Sakhalin, it grows on the plains and lower mountain slopes at elevations of 330–2970 ft. (100–900 m) above sea level. This desirable maple grows into a large, wide-spreading bush or medium-sized tree 39–50 ft. (12–15 m) high. The bark is reputed to be the roughest and most deeply fissured of any maple. The attractive, deeply divided, glossy ivy-like leaves are more deeply divided than those of the typical *A. pictum*, separating at least two-thirds way toward the leaf base. The medium-

Acer truncatum. Photo by Ray Prag.

sized leaves are mostly five-lobed often with a characteristically straight leaf base. Each triangular-ovate lobe has a long, slender, pointed tip. The center lobe may have one or a pair of broad, pointed teeth on the outer shoulder. The emerging leaves are an eye-catching red to purple shade, soon becoming glossy green for the summer, and turning to a brilliant shiny yellow-orange in the fall with red and purple. The specific name means "truncated," referring to the often flat leaf base.

'Akikaze nishiki'. The leaves have a base color of rich green which is marked with white variegations. Some leaves are all white, while others have only a few white flecks. The main pattern is white or cream cut-in a portion of the green leaf. In these leaves, the variegated portion is curved or sickle-shaped. Often the green leaf is stippled with tiny specks of white, forming a solid pattern with the green showing through from beneath. The medium-sized leaf usually has five lobes. Each lobe generally is triangular-ovate, but all lobes are irregularly curved or sickle-shaped. As new leaves emerge, the variegation has a definite pink tone which soon changes to white or cream. This cultivar forms a tall shrub, reaching up to 16 ft. (5 m) high. It is not a rapid grower and should have some protection from the hot afternoon sun.

Acer tschonoskii
Tschonoski's maple

This small graceful snakebark maple is native to Japan, growing in the subalpine mountain forests at elevations of 4550–8125 ft. (1400–1500 m) above sea level. It forms a large shrub or small tree up to 16–23 ft. (5–7 m) tall, and makes a pleasant choice in a mixed landscape. The small, round, shallowly five-lobed leaves have very coarsely toothed margins and shortly pointed tips. The leaves are green with rusty brown hairs beneath. Fall colors are yellow to gold, sometimes pink tinged, but not outstanding. This species is one of the easiest, hardiest, and most tolerant maple species to grow. It does not like alkaline soils.

Acer truncatum 'Akikaze nishiki'. Photo by J. D. Vertrees.

Acer tschonoskii. Photo by Peter Gregory.

USDA HARDINESS ZONE MAP

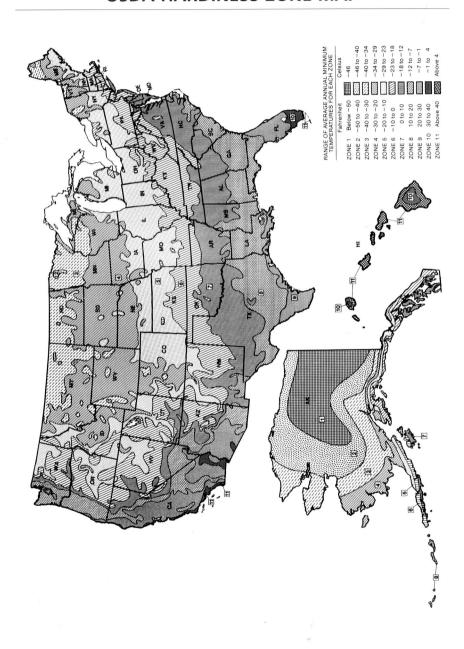

RANGE OF AVERAGE ANNUAL MINIMUM TEMPERATURES FOR EACH ZONE		
	Fahrenheit	Celsius
ZONE 1	Below −50	−46
ZONE 2	−50 to −40	−46 to −40
ZONE 3	−40 to −30	−40 to −34
ZONE 4	−30 to −20	−34 to −29
ZONE 5	−20 to −10	−29 to −23
ZONE 6	−10 to 0	−23 to −18
ZONE 7	0 to 10	−18 to −12
ZONE 8	10 to 20	−12 to −7
ZONE 9	20 to 30	−7 to −1
ZONE 10	30 to 40	−1 to 4
ZONE 11	Above 40	Above 4

EUROPEAN HARDINESS ZONE MAP

NURSERY SOURCES

This is a partial list, limited to nurseries in the United States, the United Kingdom, and Europe that specialize in Japanese maples and maples from Japan. Many of them offer hard-to-find plants. Catalogs or lists are available from most. No endorsement is intended, nor is criticism implied of sources not mentioned. Most good local garden centers usually stock a wide selection of cultivars.

Blackhawk Nursery
P.O. Box 3625
41106 Bushman Road
Quincy, California 95971
U.S.A.
(530) 283-4769
www.blackhawknursery.com

Bloom River Gardens
P.O. Box 177
Walterville, Oregon 97489
U.S.A.
(541) 726-8997
www.bloomriver.com

The Bodwen Nursery
Pothole, St. Austell
Cornwall PL26 7DW
England
44 (0)1726 883 855
www.bodwen.com

Burncoose Nurseries
Gwennap, Redruth
Cornwall TR16 6BJ
England
44 (0)1209 860316
www.burncoose.co.uk

J. Carlson Growers
8938 Newburg Road
Rockford, Illinois 61108
U.S.A.
(815) 332-5610

C.E.C.E.
Jardin Arboretum
Avenue Leopold III, 12
7130 Bray (Binche)
Belgium
32 (0)64 338 215

Choice Ornamental Plant Nursery
Hill Side
Mill Lane, Aldington, Ashford
Kent TN25 7AL
England
44 (0)1233 720 218

Credale Nursery
Upper Hill, Leominster
Herefordshire HR6 0JZ
England
44 (0)1568 720 476

Del's Japanese Maples
30050 Heather Oak Drive
Junction City, Oregon 97448
U.S.A.
(541) 688-5587

Dragon Cloud Japanese Maples
P.O. Box 815
Rocklin, California 95677
U.S.A.
(916) 847-9075

Eastwoods Nurseries
634 Long Mountain Road
Washington, Virginia 22747
U.S.A.
(540) 675-1234
www.japanesemaples.com

Fantastic Plants
5865 Steeplechase
Bartlett, Tennessee 38134
U.S.A.
(901) 438-1912
www.fantasticplants.com

Forest Farm Nursery
990 Tetherow Road
Williams, Oregon 97544
U.S.A.
(541) 846-7269
www.forestfarm.com

Fratelli Gilardelli
1-20041 Agrate Brianza
Viale delle Industrie, 21
Milan, Italy
44 (039) 653 216

Goscote Nurseries
Syston Road, Cossington
Leicestershire LE7 4UZ
England
44 (0)1509 812 121
www.goscote.co.uk

Greer Gardens
1280 Goodpasture Island Road
Eugene, Oregon 97401
U.S.A.
(541) 686-8266
www.greergardens.com

Grey Cat Farm Nursery
4610 Simmons Road
Chilliwack, B.C. V2R 4R7
Canada
(604) 823-4780

Hergest Croft Gardens
Ridgebourne, Kington
Herefordshire HR5 3EG
England
44 (0)1544 230160

Hippopottering Nursery
Orchard House
E Lound, Haxey
Doncaster DN9 2LR
England
44 (0)7979 764 677

Johnnie's Pleasure Plants
31 Ware Road
Tallassee, Alabama 36078
U.S.A.
(334) 567-7049

Kellygreen Nursery
P.O. Box 1130
Drain, Oregon 97435
U.S.A.
(800) 477-5676

Lake's Nursery
8435 Crater Hill Road
Newcastle, California 95658
U.S.A.
(530) 885-1027
www.lakesnursery.com

Dick van der Maat Entcultures
Laag-Boskoop 92
2771 gz Boskoop
Netherlands
31 172 218 337

Maillot Bonsai
Pepinieres du Bois Frazy
F01990 Relevant
France
33 (0)474 552 348
www.maillot-bonsai.com

Mallet Court Nursery
Curry Mallet, Taunton
Somerset TA3 6SY
England
44 (0)1823 481 493
www.malletcourt.co.uk

Marca Dickie Nursery
P.O. Box 1270
Boyes Hot Spring, California 95416
U.S.A.
(707) 996-0364

Mendocino Maples Nursery
41569 Little Lake Road
Mendocino, California 95460
U.S.A.
(707) 937-1189
www.mendocinomaples.com

M.G.H. Nurseries
50 Tullyhenon Road
Banbridge, County Down BT32 4EY
Northern Ireland
44 (0)2840 622 795

Miyama Asian Maples
P.O. Box 1719
Laytonville, California 95454, U.S.A.
(707) 984-8314
www.miyamaasianmaples.com

Momiji Nursery (Japanese Maples by Momiji)
2765 Stoney Point Road
Santa Rosa, California 95407
(707) 528-2917
www.momijinursery.com

Mountain Maples Nursery
P.O. Box 1329
Laytonville, California 95454
U.S.A.
(888) 707-6522
www.mountainmaples.com

Oakland Bay Nursery
5960 Highway 3
Shelton, Washington 98584
U.S.A.
(360) 427-7172

Otter Nurseries
Gosford Road
Ottery St Mary
Devon EX11 1LZ
England
44 (0)1404 815 815
www.otternurseries.co.uk

Perryhill Nurseries
Hartfield
East Sussex TN7 4JP
England
44 (0)1892 770 377
www.perryhillnurseries.co.uk

PlantenTuin Esveld
Rijneveld 72
2771 XS Boskoop
Netherlands
31 (0)172 213289
www.esveld.nl

Planten Tuin de Oirsprong
Eindhovensedijk 34b
Oirschot
Netherlands
31 (0)402 621021

P.M.A. Plant Specialities
Junker's Nursery
Lower Mead, West Hatch
Taunton
Somerset TA3 5RN
England
44 (0)1823 480 774
www.junker.co.uk

Rarefind Nursery
957 Patterson Road
Jackson, New Jersey 08527
U.S.A.
(732) 833-0613
www.rarefindnursery.com

Surry Gardens
P.O. Box 145
Surry, Maine 04684
U.S.A.
(207) 667-4493
www.surrygardens.com

Topiary Gardens
1840 Stump Road
Marcellus, New York 13108
U.S.A.
(315) 374-8125
www.topiary-gardens.com

Wells Medina Nursery
8300 NE 24th Street
Medina, Washington 98039
U.S.A.
(425) 454-1853
www.wellsmedinanursery.com

Westonbirt Arboretum Plant Centre
Westonbirt, Tetbury
Gloucestershire GL8 8QS
England
44 (0)1666 880554
www.westonbirtarboretum.com

Whitney Gardens and Nursery
P.O. Box 170
306264 Highway 101
Brinnon, Washington 98320
U.S.A.
(360) 796-4411
www.whitneygardens.com

Wildwood Farm Nursery
10300 Sonoma Highway
Kenwood, California 95452
U.S.A.
(707) 833-1161
www.wildwoodmaples.com

Zuliani Vivai Piante
via Palazzina, 2
37134 Verona
Italy
39 (0)45 505 128
www.zulianivivai.it

GLOSSARY

acuminate narrowing gradually to a point

cultivar a plant maintained solely by cultivation; a cultivated variety

fastigiate having a growth habit where branches grow upwards at an acute angle to the stem(s), tending to form a narrow, erect tree or shrub

glaucous coated with a waxy white to blue-gray bloom

lanceolate lancelike; narrow and tapering at the ends

lobulate having small leaf lobes

lobule a small leaf lobe

midrib the central main vein in a leaf or leaf lobe

obtuse blunt or rounded at the end

ovate egg-shaped

palmate shaped like a hand with fingers (leaf lobes) spread outward

pendulous bending downward, hanging

propagation increasing the number of plants, usually by cuttings, grafting, layering, or by seed

prostrate lying flat on the ground

pubescent covered in soft hairs or down

reticulated having a conspicuous network of veins

samara the single-seeded, winged fruit of the maple; usually joined in pairs

sport a mutation or abnormal growth

trifoliate of a leaf having three leaflets

truncate straight across, as when the leaf base is at right angles to the leafstalk

undulate having a wavy uneven surface

variegate a plant with bicolored or multi-colored leaves

witches' broom an abnormal growth of closely bunched, usually dwarf twigs on a branch or stem

FURTHER READING

Hardÿ de Beaulieu, Antoine le. 2003. *An Illustrated Guide to Maples*. Portland, Oregon: Timber Press.

Harris, James G. S. 2000. *The Gardener's Guide to Growing Maples*. Portland, Oregon: Timber Press.

Hillier Nurseries. 2002. *The Hillier Manual of Trees and Shrubs*. Devon, United Kingdom: David & Charles Publishers.

Lamble, G. 1997. *The Cultivation of Japanese Maples*. Privately printed.

Murphy, Michael. 2005. *A Guide to Growing Maples in Southern California*. Privately printed.

Royal Horticultural Society. 2005. *RHS Plant Finder 2005–2006*. London: Dorling Kindersley.

van Gelderen, C. J., and D. M. van Gelderen. 1999. *Maples for Gardens*. Portland, Oregon: Timber Press.

van Gelderen, D. M., P. C. de Jong, H. J. Oterdoom, and J. R. P. van Hoey Smith. 1994. *Maples of the World*. Portland, Oregon: Timber Press.

Vertrees, J. D. 2001. *Japanese Maples: Momiji and Kaede*. 3rd ed. Revised and updated by Peter Gregory. Portland, Oregon: Timber Press.

Yano, Masayoshi. 2003. *Book for Maples: Wild Maples of Japan and Maple Cultivars*. Japan Maple Publishing Group.

INDEX